Application Security for the Android
Platform

Jeff Six

O'REILLY®

Beijing · Cambridge · Farnham · Köln · Sebastopol · Tokyo

Application Security for the Android Platform
by Jeff Six

Published by O'Reilly Media, Inc., 1005 Gravenstein Highway North, Sebastopol, CA 95472.

O'Reilly books may be purchased for educational, business, or sales promotional use. Online editions are also available for most titles (*http://my.safaribooksonline.com*). For more information, contact our corporate/institutional sales department: (800) 998-9938 or *corporate@oreilly.com*.

Editors: Andy Oram and Mike Hendrickson	**Cover Designer:** Karen Montgomery
Production Editor: Melanie Yarbrough	**Interior Designer:** David Futato
Proofreader: Melanie Yarbrough	**Illustrator:** Robert Romano

Revision History for the First Edition:

    2011-12-02   First release

See *http://oreilly.com/catalog/errata.csp?isbn=9781449315078* for release details.

ISBN: 978-1-449-31507-8

[LSI]

1322594901

Table of Contents

Preface

The purpose of this book is to convey vital knowledge about application security to developers working on the Android platform, to enable the development of robust, rugged, and more secure applications.

While application security knowledge and skills have matured rapidly over the past couple of years, that knowledge is still scattered in a huge number of diverse locations. As of now, no single resource has existed that a developer with some experience in developing Android applications could turn to in order to understand the more important topics within the application security space and to find guidance on how to make their applications more secure. If you are such a developer, you'll find the key points of application security that you need to know to develop secure applications laid out in a succinct and actionable manner. If you are an experienced security engineer or practitioner, you'll find a summary of the unique characteristics of Android that you need to know to work within this environment. In short, this book enables the development of secure applications for the Android platform, whatever your background.

Organization of the Book

Although the chapters cover different topics, they have been arranged so that the concepts and techniques in earlier chapters form a foundation for the others.

Chapter 1, *Introduction*
Lays out the importance of this topic, and perhaps scares you a bit, so as to motivate you to read the book.

Chapter 2, *Android Architecture*
Describes the way Android differs from other common systems, notably desktop systems, and how its architecture both enables security and requires you to work with its unique structure.

Chapter 3, *Application Permissions*
Looks behind the familiar list of permissions that users see when adding applications to their devices, and shows how to use the system robustly without overwhelming the user.

Chapter 4, *Component Security and Permissions*

Takes the permissions system to a finer granularity by showing how components such as Content Providers and Services can grant limited access to their data and functions.

Chapter 5, *Protecting Stored Data*

Treats the critical topic of encrypting data so that it is secure even if the user or a thief can bypass other application security controls provided by Android (or when such controls do not apply).

Chapter 6, *Securing Server Interactions*

Shows how you can protect the interactions between your application and the servers it communicates with.

Chapter 7, *Summary*

Focuses on the key take-aways from the book.

Conventions Used in This Book

The following typographical conventions are used in this book:

Italic

Indicates new terms, URLs, email addresses, filenames, and file extensions.

`Constant width`

Used for program listings, as well as within paragraphs to refer to program elements such as variable or function names, databases, data types, and environment variables.

`Constant width bold`

Shows commands or other text that should be typed literally by the user.

`Constant width italic`

Shows text that should be replaced with user-supplied values or by values determined by context.

 This icon signifies a tip, suggestion, or general note.

 This icon indicates a warning or caution.

Using Code Examples

This book is here to help you get your job done. In general, you may use the code in this book in your programs and documentation. You do not need to contact us for permission unless you're reproducing a significant portion of the code. For example, writing a program that uses several chunks of code from this book does not require permission. Selling or distributing a CD-ROM of examples from O'Reilly books does require permission. Answering a question by citing this book and quoting example code does not require permission. Incorporating a significant amount of example code from this book into your product's documentation does require permission.

We appreciate, but do not require, attribution. An attribution usually includes the title, author, publisher, and ISBN. For example: "*Application Security for the Android Platform* by Jeff Six (O'Reilly). Copyright 2012 Jeff Six, 978-1-449315-078."

If you feel your use of code examples falls outside fair use or the permission given above, feel free to contact us at *permissions@oreilly.com*.

Safari® Books Online

 Safari Books Online is an on-demand digital library that lets you easily search over 7,500 technology and creative reference books and videos to find the answers you need quickly.

With a subscription, you can read any page and watch any video from our library online. Read books on your cell phone and mobile devices. Access new titles before they are available for print, and get exclusive access to manuscripts in development and post feedback for the authors. Copy and paste code samples, organize your favorites, download chapters, bookmark key sections, create notes, print out pages, and benefit from tons of other time-saving features.

O'Reilly Media has uploaded this book to the Safari Books Online service. To have full digital access to this book and others on similar topics from O'Reilly and other publishers, sign up for free at *http://my.safaribooksonline.com*.

How to Contact Us

Please address comments and questions concerning this book to the publisher:

> O'Reilly Media, Inc.
> 1005 Gravenstein Highway North
> Sebastopol, CA 95472
> 800-998-9938 (in the United States or Canada)
> 707-829-0515 (international or local)
> 707-829-0104 (fax)

We have a web page for this book, where we list errata, examples, and any additional information. You can access this page at:

http://www.oreilly.com/catalog/9781449315078

To comment or ask technical questions about this book, send email to:

bookquestions@oreilly.com

For more information about our books, courses, conferences, and news, see our website at *http://www.oreilly.com*.

Find us on Facebook: *http://facebook.com/oreilly*

Follow us on Twitter: *http://twitter.com/oreillymedia*

Watch us on YouTube: *http://www.youtube.com/oreillymedia*

Acknowledgments

Many thanks to the technical reviewers, who provided valuable comments on early drafts of the book.

- Miguel Azevedo
- Drew Hintz
- Masumi Nakamura
- Members of the Android team at Google

The author would like to thank his wife, Cindy, for keeping him grounded and sane during the development of this book.

CHAPTER 1

Introduction

Welcome, developer! This book is for you: software developers that write for the Android mobile platform. Here you will learn what you need to know about the world of application security, and the interaction between software development and information security. In today's world, application security knowledge is one thing that can differentiate developers.

Like it or not, you will be releasing applications into a high-threat environment. Although the Android platform is still pretty new and offers lots of great opportunities, it is also routinely targeted by malicious hackers who want to compromise mobile applications—your mobile applications—for their own gain (note that this is not to say that Android is targeted any more than other systems, such as web browsers, document formats, and so on; any platform with a decent number of users is a target nowadays, and Android sure has that). This book will teach you the basics of how to design and implement secure, robust, and rugged applications on the Android platform. It will also teach you how malicious hackers may view your application and how they may choose to attack it, information you can put to good use when designing and implementing your app.

As noted, this book is targeted to developers who are already developing for the Android mobile platform, or plan to. It assumes you have a decent knowledge of the Android environment, including how to design, build, and deploy applications. It does not, however, assume any background in application security, cryptography, or secure software development. What you, as a developer, need to know about these topics is exactly what this book aims to provide. This book exists to give you the information you need —no more, no less—to effectively develop in this environment.

Finally, before we get started—thanks. Thank you for taking an interest in application security and making the effort to increase your knowledge of how to create secure, robust, and rugged applications. The only way the current state of vulnerable, constantly exploited applications will change is for developers to see the need for more secure development practices and knowledge, and by their gaining that knowledge. Welcome to that journey.

Application Security: Why You Should Care

Security...why should you, as a developer, care? Security, in the context of information technology, refers to things like firewalls, intrusion detection systems, antivirus programs, and things like that. Surely someone who writes general purpose applications like games, calendaring apps, and photo manipulation tools does not need to worry about security, right? Wrong!

Imagine that you write apps to help busy people manage their schedules, and that you take advantage of cloud services to make that information available to your customers on their Android smartphones and tablets anywhere they go. This is a very useful service and many of the people who take advantage of it will be those who are very busy: financial services executives, for example. Your app takes off and sees widespread adoption. Then a busy executive is chatting with a friend from another firm at a conference and lets it slip that his firm has been reading the executive's calendar. They have been able to see whom this executive was meeting with, what potential deals the firm was working on, and other confidential information! After some investigation, the executive learns that your calendaring app is vulnerable to what the application security field calls a command injection vulnerability, and that an unscrupulous engineer at his firm's competitor has discovered this and was using it to target the competition's mobile devices to grab sensitive information.

Let's consider another situation: you write a really cool app that allows people to access many of their social media accounts all from one place. Users are able to see updates from their connections on Facebook, Google+, Twitter, and whatever other networks and services will emerge in the near future, all in one place. Users love this tool and use it all the time. Things are going great until you get an email one morning from a user who complains that all of her social media account details, including her passwords, have been published on a site hosted in eastern Europe. You check out the site and sure enough, details for thousands of users are posted. Looking through your accounting records, they are all users of your integration app. The next email you receive confirms your fears. It is from the hacker who stole this data. He reveals that he snuck a bit of code into an Android app that he released that looked, for unsecured database instances, like the one your app used, and grabbed all that data. Now, if you do not want him to release all of that information publicly, a large "protection fee" will be required.

Whose fault are these situations? Yours! You did not fully appreciate the environment that mobile applications run in. Gone are the days when you could deploy insecure, poorly developed code and no one cared. Now you are releasing your code to what we call a high-threat environment, more commonly known as the Internet. Your software is running on a device that has an always-on Internet connection and runs your code along with hundreds of other apps, all of which are from different authors, some of whom are anonymous. You failed to account for unexpected data to arrive over the network in the first example, and you failed to properly secure the sensitive data you were storing from other apps on the device in the second.

Pure developer anonymity is not entirely possible, as anyone uploading applications into the Android Market is required to supply a valid credit card and corresponding identity information as part of the registration process. So there is some degree of assurance there. However, since it is possible—pretty easy in fact—to allow installation of applications from other sources (and there are a lot of third-party applications stores out there) on Android devices, this identity property only applies to applications obtained from the official source, the Android Market.

So, who needs to worry about properly coding their applications to resist such threats? Easy: anyone who is coding any application at all. Every single developer needs to have a basic understanding of application security. You need to understand why it is important to restrict access to certain components of your application, such as your database. You need to understand what cryptography is and how you can use different cryptographic functions to provide appropriate protections to the data your app is storing and processing. You need to understand how the Android environment works and how apps can be written that are secure, robust, and rugged. Luckily for you, all of these topics will be discussed in this book. We will get you up to speed with what you need to know as a developer. Your code, and the protection you are offering to your customers' data, will be much better off for it.

The Current State of Mobile Application Security on Android

As of late 2011, the Android ecosystem has an awful lot going for it. Android phones are extremely popular and new models seem to come out every couple of days. There are thousands upon thousands of apps in the Android Market and the Java-based development model is appealing to lots of developers. Google continues to innovate on this platform at a rapid pace; indeed, Android 4.0, Ice Cream Sandwich, should be available by the time this book is published. This should resolve the current incompatibilities between phone and tablet versions.

However, all is not well in the world of Android. Recent analysis by outside firms has found multiple types of malware embedded in apps released on the Android Market. A lot more malware has been found in other, non-Google application stores. Tricking the user into installing the app by posing as a useful tool or game, the software then steals data from the phone and sends it out to unknown people with unknown motivations.

Some examples of malicious Android apps, discovered and removed from the Market, are:

- Super Guitar Solo
- Photo Editor
- Advanced Currency Converter

- Spider Man
- Hot Sexy Videos

People will try all sorts of things, making their malicious code look like all varieties of legitimate apps, in order to get unsuspecting users to install and run them. All of these examples were available on the Android Market and downloaded by many users before they were pulled. Indeed, this spoofing of legitimate applications and legitimate functions is not unique to Android Market either; it is a trait of any large scale system.

Android was designed from the ground up with a strong security model, so has that model been effective in mitigating this type of threat? The fact that this malware exists indicates that it has not, nor could anything really ever be, a panacea for platform security. And while this threat does continue to exist, the sandbox/permissions approach has provided some key wins. First, it does reduce the scope of functionality for most applications (reducing the attack surface for the malware if it does get to run on a device). The permissions model also provides users with better information about the real behavior of the applications they are installing, and combined with user reviews and feedback through the Android Market (and other sources), users can research to detect malicious applications. Finally, the malware that has been seen is more limited in its scope than that which exists for other platforms (although some malware actually exploits vulnerabilities in the Android system itself to obtain root-level access and do really nasty things). So, while the threat of malware on Android is real and will continue to be so, the security model, composed of the permissions capability and other constructs, does provide some real benefits and protection for the users.

In addition to these Android platform-specific troubles, it seems that every day brings news of a compromise of private data, with hacker groups releasing stolen files and large security firms announcing that they have discovered massive penetrations of huge numbers of corporations with industrial espionage (the stealing of corporate secrets) as the goal. Now, let's note that these actions have occurred against computer systems in general; large-scale compromise of data like this has not been seen from Android platforms. Though the computer security industry has come a very long way in its short lifetime, things are clearly not working very well and the need for developers to release software that is less vulnerable is easily apparent.

Security: Risk = Vulnerability + Threat + Consequences

Security is all about managing risk. You will never ever have a perfectly secure system. The most honest statements ever made about being 100% sure that your information is secure is known as Richards' Law of Computer Security, which dates from 1992[*]. The first law: don't buy a computer. The second law: if you do buy a computer, don't

---

[*] Source: http://virusbusters.itcs.umich.edu/um- resources/vb-interview.html (*http://virusbusters.itcs.umich .edu/um- resources/vb-interview.html*)

turn it on. That is very useful and practical advice, no? Seriously, application security is all about tradeoffs. Think back to the example discussed in the previous section, centered on a social media integration app. If we need perfect assurance, a 100% guarantee, that the user's usernames and passwords would not be compromised, the only way to accomplish this would be to not store them at all. However, this would make the entire concept of our application infeasible. We need to take on some risk in order to provide any useful services.

Compare this to a real-world example. Credit cards can be stolen, and if your card is stolen and used by the thief, you may need to go through some time-consuming and annoying processes to recover. When you hand your credit card to your waiter at a restaurant to settle your bill, there is a chance that he will run that card through a skimming device back in the kitchen that would allow him to clone that card and use it fraudulently. The only way to prevent this attack from occurring, with 100% certainty, is to not ever use your credit cards in any manner where they leave your sight (indeed, this is how things are handled in Europe, where waiters bring the card processing machine to your table...but could you spot a card skimmer attached to such a machine?). You incur some risk when you hand that card over. However, you also incur a benefit in that you do not need to carry cash to pay for your meal, you obtain some rewards points from your card company, and you obtain a useful itemized statement of all your purchases every month. In modern society, most people have decided that these rewards outweigh the risk and are willing to hand over their credit card.

How is this decision made? How do we know whether the reward is worth the risk? The first thing we need to understand is what risk is. There are three primary components of risk: *vulnerability*, *threat*, and *consequences*. Let's look at each of these three to see where risk comes from.

A *vulnerability* is something that allows an unintended and undesirable action to take place. In our credit card example, the vulnerability is that our credit card leaves our sight and we have no control over what happens to it at that point (one may also note that having a universally authenticated identification method, like a credit card number, is also a vulnerability in this scenario; why is the knowledge of a credit card number accepted as sufficient proof that you are whomever that card number belongs to?). The widespread availability of card skimmers is also a component of the vulnerability; if the card could not be duplicated in so quick and easy of a manner, the situation would be less concerning.

A *threat* is the second component of risk. A threat is something, or someone, that can take advantage of a vulnerability. In this case, the threat is a waiter who does take the card and clone it, using it to make fraudulent purchases. Here, we can judge that the threat is probably somewhat low. Most waiters are honest, hardworking people, so the threat in this case is much lower than what it may be if we were using that card to pay for stolen electronics instead of a meal, as an individual selling stolen goods is much more likely to steal our card information as well. So while the vulnerability in this situation may be severe, the threat is not particularly high.

The third component of risk is *consequence*. This refers to what would happen if whatever bad things we are considering were to actually happen. If we hand over our credit card to the waiter and he skims it and clones the card, what are the consequences? If no mitigations were in place (more about that in a second), the attacker could quickly purchase thousands of dollars worth of goods that we could then be charged for, potentially ruining our credit and requiring many hours of painful work to get resolved. The consequences of having our credit card cloned, through a successful exploitation of the vulnerability by the threat, could be severe.

What do we have here with regard to risk? The current system has a pretty serious vulnerability in it, as the card leaves our sight and can be easily cloned with the right device (which is widely available to anyone that wants one). The threat is probably pretty low, as most waiters are not out to steal our card information. The consequences of such a successful exploitation, however, could be pretty high. Consider all of these factors together and we can get a decent idea of what the risk of paying for our meal with a credit card is, and it is not a particularly positive outcome. This is basic definition of risk; it is a function of vulnerability, threat, and consequences.

So why are people are willing to hand over their cards on a regular basis? The risk is not at the level we have just calculated. The parties that are involved have implemented mitigations to reduce that risk. As we have seen, risk is a function of vulnerability, threat, and consequences. If the severity of any of these three can be reduced, the overall risk will go down. In our example, credit card companies have done a lot to mitigate the consequences to the consumer. In the United States, liability (what you are responsible for paying) for charges made on a compromised card is capped at $50 and many card companies set that value to zero. So if a customer were to charge their meal and the card were cloned and used fraudulently, the customer would not be responsible for the charge and such occurrences would not negatively impact the customer's credit rating. The credit card companies take on that risk themselves because they need to reduce the consequences of credit card compromise in order to bring the risk (to the consumer) associated with using the cards down to an acceptable level. Because the actual consequences of a compromise are very slight, customers do not hesitate to use their cards, as the level of risk is greatly reduced due to this mitigation.

Think about the credit card example a bit—what other mitigations could be applied to this example to reduce the vulnerability, threat, or consequences? You can probably come up with quite a few.

A Short Bit on Device and User Account Security

It is possible, and in some cases very desirable, for your application to learn about the security status of the device it is running on. Using the Device Management API, introduced in Android 2.2, applications can determine password policies on devices, determine if device encryption capabilities are enabled, and other similar functions. These capabilities are useful in some situations, but are somewhat outside the scope of this book. Nevertheless, should you have a need to determine or influence the state of some of the device's security features, it is good to know this API exists, so consider yourself so informed.

One other important and related topic is the security of a Google account. Android devices are almost always tied to a Google account and the Google services provided by Android applications typically use that account. It is, therefore, very important to keep your Google account safe and inaccessible by anyone else. Google provides a number of security features that can, and should, be enabled. These include the ability to require two-factor authentication to access your account (you need to know your password and also type in a code sent to your mobile phone when you attempt to log in), configuring a secondary email address to enable account recovery, and so on. So much within Android is tied to this Google account that its security should be a top priority.

Evolution of Information Security: Why Applications Matter the Most

One who practices security has to worry about a great number of things. The fundamental field generally focuses on providing three services: *confidentiality*, *integrity*, and *availability* (CIA). *Confidentiality* refers to making sure that only those people (or devices, or systems, etc.) that are supposed to have access to certain information have it. For example, in the social media integration app example we have been discussing, the stored usernames and passwords should be available only to that one app and the respective service the users belong to. *Integrity* refers to making sure that data is not altered by anyone who should not be doing so. In the calendaring app we have discussed, a bit of hidden code in a game installed on a phone should not be able to change the user's appointment schedule, causing him to miss important meetings. *Availability* refers to ensuring that services are functioning as they should; for example, an attacker sending lots and lots of bogus requests to a server should not be able to disrupt that service for legitimate users. This CIA triad is a very general and very simplistic model for what applications need to protect.

Application security is a big deal nowadays. Fifteen years ago, the main subject of interest was the operating system. In the late 1990s, attackers constantly discovered and exploited conditions known as *buffer overflows* in Unix-based systems and services (we will discuss buffer overflows in general a bit later). In the early 2000s, the target switched to desktop operating systems, specifically Windows XP, where a large amount of vulnerabilities were found that allowed attackers full access to systems, including the ability to read, change, or destroy the data contained within. Indeed, even as Windows Vista was being developed at the same time Windows XP was being exploited so rapidly, Microsoft put a freeze in place on Vista development to focus efforts on fixing XP's security. It took them a long time, but Microsoft has come a very long way to producing solid, secure, robust, rugged code. Modern Windows operating systems are much less exploitable than previous versions.

This success in strengthening the operating system causes attackers to move on to other targets. For a while, network devices such as switches and routers were the preferred targets, and then applications. If the operating system that an application runs on was much harder to exploit, what about the application itself? It had access to the data on the system and a whole lot more people write applications than operating systems. So the expertise that operating system developers gained writing code with fewer vulnerabilities, and the mitigation against the consequences of a successful exploit, was in far less supply at the application level. Due to these factors, applications are targeted all of the time now. Attackers have moved from the once vulnerability-filled environment of the operating system to the still vulnerability-filled environment of the application. You, as an application developer, need to be ready for them.

Your Role: Protect the Data

You write the apps. The apps need to process some data. Attackers want to do bad things—steal, alter, or block access to—that data. When a user chooses to use your app, they trust you with all of the data they supply. They also trust that your application is written correctly so that none of the other data stored on their device will be compromised by letting your app run on it as well. If you write apps and you want people to use them, you need to do your best to safeguard your customers. Your job is simple: write your applications so that they do what their users expect them to do, no more and no less. Carrying out that job is less simple.

The first order of business is for you to understand how Android works. If you are writing apps to run on this platform, you need to understand how your apps will, or will not, interact with other apps on the device and with the system itself. You need to understand how you can store data within Android's SQLite datastore and how to secure that data so that only your app can access it. If it is sensitive data, such as passwords, email, or other things that your customers would not want to be compromised, you need to understand why you may need to protect it more fully (such as utilizing cryptography) and how you would do so using Android's built-in capabilities. You also need to understand the permissions model and how you can let a user know what permissions your app will need, and then make an informed decision as to whether they will allow it to do so (why does this game I just downloaded need full access to my SMS messages, anyway?). And the list goes on and on.

Now you may be saying at this point, "This is a lot of things to learn...I just want to write some apps!" and you would be right. Application security is an involved topic and requires a good amount of practice to master. But it is also an area where a little knowledge goes a long way. Once you understand the basics, you will pick up on more and more, faster and faster. Once you start thinking about security, you will do so more and more, growing into a certain mindset where you are evaluating risk, and designing and implementing mitigations, before you even realize what you are doing. You will identify and resolve potential vulnerabilities before you even code them up. You will protect the data.

Secure Software Development Techniques

As Microsoft learned many years ago when dealing with a large amount of exploitations against Windows XP, it can be quite hard to build secure code. With some exceptions, developers are not taught to think of security as part of their formal training. As the need for this type of information and training has become more and more evident, companies have developed application security training for their in-house developers, organizations such as the Open Web Application Security Project (OWASP) have emerged to develop open source training, and universities have begun offering application security courses in their computer science curriculums. Books, such as the very one you are reading, provide great information so that developers can quickly get up to speed on creating more secure applications. However, developer education only goes so far. Security is not something that you can learn about, apply to writing better code, and then forget about. Security is a process and is part of an application's entire development lifecycle.

Many large software development firms have formal Secure Software Development Life Cycles (SSDLCs), where security engineers work with developers through the entire process. All developers are trained to think about security concepts and engineers who specialize in application security add even more experience to the process. Security personnel participate in the requirements and planning phases, review source code as it is developed and submitted, perform penetration testing against the application before it is released, and analyze and repair security issues that are reported post-release.

Recent development techniques such as agile development, pair programming, and extreme programming have proven that developers work better and generate fewer errors when they work in pairs or small groups. Having multiple pairs of eyeballs on code, looking for flaws, is a great way to catch security issues that a single developer might miss, which is why those trained in secure coding (as you will be!) often perform source code analysis to find problems before those who might attack the software.

Penetration testing is a standard technique that some choose to deploy against their software, especially those that have a high degree of risk.† During such testing, the testers act in the role of attackers and attempt to study and compromise the application, much as a malicious hacker would, which is why penetration testing is sometimes known as *ethical hacking*. The combination of source code and design review with

---

† For example, an application that allows individuals to trade stocks they own has a high risk. Why do you think that is: does such an application have high vulnerability, threat, and/or consequences associated with it?

penetration testing has proven to be very successful in finding and correcting security issues with applications.

As you can see, producing a secure application can be very time-consuming and can require a lot of education, careful consideration, and a variety of testing techniques. This really comes down to one simple observation: programming is hard! Programming code that does not have errors is pretty much impossible. Programming code that does not have errors that can be exploited by malicious hackers to compromise that application, a subset of the problem, has proven to be quite hard by itself. The extent of these techniques that you may need to employ for your applications is all a matter of risk management; the amount of work taken to secure your application must be appropriate based on the risk. If you are developing a standalone mobile game that will not process or store any data or use any protected Android APIs like network communications, both the threat against your app and the consequences of a successful exploitation are probably pretty low. In such a case, you may judge that the small risk that your game is exposed to is acceptable, an appropriate *risk acceptance*. On the other hand, if you are writing the social media integration app we have talked about, there is a high threat targeting your app because social media credentials are sought after by malicious hackers. The consequences are somewhat high because the compromise of your users' credentials would be a very negative thing for you. Therefore, you may choose to employ many of the secure development techniques we have just discussed to find and fix as many vulnerabilities in your app as you can to mitigate some of that risk.

Remember, security is all about risk management and acceptance of the residual risk (the level that still exists after you have mitigated the risk as far as you can). You can never be sure you're building a 100% secure app, at least not one that does anything useful.

Unique Characteristics of Android

Android is a very interesting platform with some traits that clearly separate it from other mobile platforms.

One of the most representative features of the Android ecosystem is the open development model. Google allows any developer to put their apps on the Android Market, after they have registered as an Android developer. This requires the developer to pay a small fee with a credit card so there is some assurance that a real person is at the other end of the chain, and there is some accountability for that person. Contrary to some popular belief, Google does scan and conduct analysis of apps throughout their Android Market lifecycle looking for malicious activity. In addition, it does find and remove applications that do bad things. When something does escape this process undetected (for example, malware that misrepresents itself and includes functionality that is not always bad but only bad in this context—think a game that also attempts to read your SMS messages and send them off to somewhere over the Internet), this is where the Android permissions system comes in to play. Every Android app must declare which restricted system APIs it uses and that list of permissions is presented to the user when they install the app. As a developer, the app permissions system is very important for you to understand, and as someone interested in security, it is even more important. This system can also be used to allow other apps access to certain parts of your app, whether interactive portions, background services, or databases. How this system works, the weaknesses of it, and how you as a developer will utilize it, will be discussed in great detail in later chapters.

Open and Closed Markets

An open question is, if application stores that are more open (like the Android Market) or more closed (Apple's iOS Appstore) are better in terms of security and preventing malware from reaching users. The manual review that Apple forces upon applications before they appear in the store catches applications that do things Apple does not want them to do, including many malicious actions. Google's automated, nonmanual review approach is a little more free-for-all. However, there have been applications that have slipped through the Apple process (for example, there was an approved flashlight app that also turned on tethering on an iOS device, something Apple does not allow). Also, the manual review process slows down how quickly developers can release patches and fixes for their applications, as each such release requires a full manual review. This can be bad if a developer needs to fix a security vulnerability in their code and actually reduces the overall security of the platform because of a lack of timely application patching.

Indeed, when looking at malware discovered for the Android platform, most current malware is found on third-party application stores and not the Android Market. The worst offenders (for example, the malware that attempts exploits to obtain root-level access) are found almost exclusively at distribution centers outside of the Market. While more open than the closed model, the open model of the Android Market has done a pretty good job of keeping malware off of the platform, especially when users obtain their applications exclusively from it. The freedom to choose to acquire applications from other stores, while part of the open design principles of Android, does sacrifice some of the security offered by the Market, which is why the ability to load applications from other sources is turned off by default. As always, especially when dealing with less-than-reputable sellers (or free sources), caveat emptor!

Just like most questions, the answer to which method is better for security is not straightforward and both approaches require some tradeoffs. Neither approach is obviously superior to the other, and each offers its own pros and cons.

Android devices also have the capability to be rooted. As you will see in Chapter 2, the underlying base of Android is the Linux kernel. This design prevents one app from accessing data held by another app. The Android platform also enforces the permission system that prevents one app from accessing resources, such as files and databases, of other apps. However, if a user (or someone who has stolen a phone and has access to it) wants to, full access to the device can be readily obtained (with some level of effort, which depends on a number of things). If you have a Linux background, you know that the root user can access anything on the system.

Note that there are complexities involved in rooting an Android device that are more complex than this brief treatment can fully cover. While a user can obtain root-level access if they desire, they must have access to the device (stealing a device without being able to access/unlock it, for example, would make this process quite difficult). I do not mean to imply that one can simply grab a locked Android device, connect it to something, and obtain a root shell on it. And while Android makes this process somewhat easier than other, more closed platforms, the same things can be done with those other platforms, such as jailbreaking an iOS device. While some users do root their devices, most users do not and assuming those users properly protect their device using lock-screens and strong passwords, this risk is largely mitigated.

Everything Is a System

It is important to keep in mind that nothing exists in a vacuum. For example, we have just talked about needing to consider the rooting of Android devices when performing a risk analysis for your application, something that is clearly not part of a normal, vanilla development process. However, that trait of the Android environment is something you need to consider as your application will run in that environment. Along similar lines, if your app does a lot of web interaction, perhaps using the WebKit capabilities of Android, you need to make sure you implement that portion of your system securely as well (you need to properly handle cookies, use HTTP POST instead of GET when submitting sensitive data, etc.). Those aspects are not directly covered in this book, as we are dealing with application security issues revolving around the application running on the device, but you need to keep them in mind when thinking about how your application really runs as part of a system.

Moving On

With mobile platforms growing at an unbelievable rate and the accelerating adoption of cloud services, where data will live on servers and be accessed from anywhere, the apps that run on these mobile devices must be secure, robust, and rugged. They must resist attacks as history has shown that attackers follow where the data is and they go where they can get at it. That line of battle is shifting to mobile platforms. You, as an Android developer, will be on the front lines. Your software will be attacked. It's just a matter of when. To properly defend against this, you need to understand application security and how to properly develop your apps in a secure manner.

Let's get started.

CHAPTER 2

Android Architecture

Mobile platforms have both advantages and disadvantages in relation to traditional desktop and server platforms. On the disadvantage side, mobile platforms typically have much less computing power at their disposal, less memory, fewer processor capabilities, and less mass storage. However, on the advantage side, they benefit from designers having learned from decades of experience. In addition, users expect very different things from the mobile and desktop worlds. Basically, mobile platforms and desktop (or server) platforms are distinct environments for application development.

One of the primary differences between desktop platforms and mobile platforms is the context under which applications run. On desktop platforms such as Microsoft Windows and Linux, applications typically run as the user who starts them. (Yes, there are provisions in both environments to run applications as separate user accounts, but this is the exception for desktop environments.) So if you install a game and run it, it runs with the same set of permissions that you have. That game would be allowed by the operating system to access your financial files, your Internet history, and your photo library just because it runs as you and gets to act as you, from the operating system's perspective. This can be especially harmful since Windows users have traditionally run as Administrator, with full privileges on the system.

In the Android world, things work somewhat differently. Each application runs as a separate user, thus changing the model that one must apply to security. Think about major desktop compromises over the past couple of years: did someone attack your PDF reader application to read your document? No, they attacked it because it ran under your account and your account could access your sensitive files. What if that PDF reader ran under its own account that had no access to anything except downloaded PDF files? The risk assessment for that app might be significantly different. We will now explore how this is one-app/one-user model is implemented under Android, the security model that results, and what this means from a developer perspective.

Introduction to the Android Architecture

The Android platform is built like pretty much every other platform: as a stack with various layers running on top of each other, lower-level layers providing services to upper-level services. In order to understand how Android is put together, let's look briefly at each of the primary layers in the Android system.

At the very bottom is the kernel, Linux. This Linux kernel is responsible for most of the things that are usually delegated to the operating system kernel, in this case mostly hardware abstraction. This is the layer where all of the device-specific hardware drivers will run, enabling hardware vendors to develop drivers in a familiar environment. This layer also enforces some of the most basic separation between apps, so we will visit it in more detail in the next section.

On top of the kernel are the native libraries. These are modules of code that are compiled down to native machine code for the device and provide some of the common services that are available for apps and other programs. They include the Surface Manager (responsible for graphics on the device's screen), 2D and 3D graphics libraries, WebKit (the web rendering engine that powers the default browser), and SQLite (the basic datastore technology for the Android platform). These native libraries run as processes within the underlying Linux kernel.

Also running as processes within the Linux kernel is the app runtime. Each app runs in its own instance of the Android runtime, and the core of each instance is a Dalvik Virtual Machine (VM). The Dalvik VM is a mobile-optimized virtual machine, specifically designed to run fast on the devices that Android targets. Also present at this layer, and in each app's runtime, are the Android core libraries, such as the Android class libraries, I/O, and other similar things.

At the next layer up the stack is the application framework. Here we find code compiled for and running on Dalvik VMs that provides services to multiple apps. Running at this level are entities such as the Package Manager, responsible for managing apps on the phone, and the Activity Manager, which is responsible for loading Activities and managing the Activity stack. Anyone can write code that runs within the application framework; a good example is an app that shares out information to other apps as a Content Provider (more about these, and how to make sure only the apps you want to access your data do so, is coming up).

Finally, apps run at the top layer. This includes apps that you write as a developer, and those that Google and other Android developers do as well. Typically, apps running at this layer include one or more of four different types of components: Activities, Broadcast Receivers, Services, and Content Providers. More about these, and the challenges of securing each of them, will be discussed shortly.

The Linux Security Model

Linux is at the heart of the Android system and much of the Android security model is a result of that. So, let's consider the Linux security model.

Central to Linux security is the concept of users and groups. Each user in a Linux system is assigned a user ID (UID) when they are created. This is just a number and is used to differentiate one user from another. In addition, users can be added to groups and each group has a group ID (GID), which is just another number used to differentiate one group from another. A user can be a member of multiple groups and each group can have multiple members.

Permissions are assigned to each resource on a Linux system, with a resource typically being a file (almost everything in Linux is viewed as a file). Each resource has a defined owner, which is the UID of the user that has primary responsibility for the file and can alter the permissions on it. Each resource also has a defined group, which is the GID of the group of users who have a set of permissions over and above that of the world, which is the group of all users on the system.

Each resource on a Linux system has three sets of permissions: owner, group, and world. So one file will have a set of permissions that apply to its owner, a set of permissions that apply to its group, and a set of permissions that apply to anyone that is not the owner or in the group that the resource is associated with (i.e. everyone else that has an account on the system). Each set of permissions can include read (R), which allows that entity to read the file; write (W), which allows that entity to write/update the file; and execute (X), which allows that file to be executed as runnable code. Note that having read permission does not imply you have write permission, and vice versa (it is entirely possible to have write permission but not read permission on a certain resource). Linux permissions are also based on the idea that if you are not granted a certain right, you do not have it. So if a specific file has read and write access set for the owner and the group, but no permissions set for the world, if you are not the owner or in the file's group, you have no access to it.

The Resulting Android Security Model

As you can see, central to the Linux security model is the concept of user IDs and group IDs. Each user that can log in to and use a Linux system is assigned a user ID (UID) and each user ID may be a member of one of more group IDs (GIDs). Because Android uses Linux as its underlying kernel, these concepts apply.

When an Android package is installed, a new user ID (one that is not currently in use on the device) is created and the new app runs under that UID. In addition, all data stored by that application is assigned that same UID, whether a file, database, or other resource. The Linux permissions on resources for that app are set to allow full permission by the associated UID and no permissions otherwise. Note that this UID is unique to the device; there is no guarantee (or even expectation) that the same UID will be used for the same application on different devices. Linux prevents apps that have different UIDs from accessing data, or otherwise accessing the process or memory, of other apps, thus providing the basis for the separation between apps on the Android platform. This concept is known as the *separation of concerns*.

Each app is pretty well separated from others by default. The underlying Linux security model, based on user IDs more than anything else, has stood the test of time. Android introduces the capability for software components to run under the same user IDs, and also as part of the same processes, which is a topic we will discuss in detail later in this chapter, but you need to know what you are doing to enable this. Another potential trouble spot comes up when you consider storing data on removable media like SD cards. A good rule of thumb, for this and other capabilities that erode the separation model is this: don't do it unless you understand the ramifications and absolutely need to do so. Otherwise, stick with the separation that is part of Android; it was designed this way—to isolate apps—for good reason!

Native Code

As we have just seen, normal Android apps run in separate processes and each runs inside of a separate Dalvik Virtual Machine. However, any app can include native code, which is code that runs outside of the Dalvik VM and is compiled to run directly on the processor within the Android device. The inclusion of native code within an Android app does not alter the security model. The same architectural separations between apps, along with the entire Android permissions system that we will discuss in Chapters 3 and 4, is enforced regardless of the type of app (Dalvik, native, or a mix of the two).

Application Signing, Attribution, and Attestation

Android apps are digitally signed. Let's now explore this concept in detail, as who signs an application will drive our ability to configure how apps can interact with each other.

A digital signature, in this context, is a cryptographic construct that a developer applies to a piece of software to prove she wrote it. We will discuss the cryptography behind this later, but for now, think of a digital signature as the technology-enabled version of your handwritten signature: you apply it to a document (or app, in this case) to identify yourself as the author, and it is very hard for anyone else to forge such a signature.

Two concepts make this work. First, a *digital certificate* identifies each developer. Think of a digital certificate like your driver's license, which establishes your identity and includes a copy of your handwritten signature that someone else can compare against a document you just signed to demonstrate that you are in fact the person identified on the license. The other part to this process is your *private key*. This is really just a very long number that you can use to generate the actual signature. It's critical to this process that your private key is known only by you; if someone else were to obtain it, they could generate a digital signature that identifies the author as you, just as you could. So for a digital signature to work, you need your own private key to sign the app in question and a matching digital certificate, which other people can use to verify your signature and see that the app was, in fact, authored by you.

Typically, these constructs (digital certificates and the associated private keys) are one of two different types. The first type are certificates created by Certificate Authorities (CAs). Think of a CA as the Department of Motor Vehicles that issues you a driver's license. You must prove to them that you are the person in question before they will grant you a license with that identity on it. Everyone has agreed that they will trust the DMV to do a decent job at this, so if your license comes from the DMV and it has your name on it, people will trust that it is really you. A CA will make you prove that you really are the developer in question before it will issue you a digital certificate with your identity on it (and the associate private key). As in the driver's license example, assuming you have agreed to trust the CA in question, you can trust that the identity on the digital certificate is, in fact, correct and has been verified by the CA.

The other type of certificate is a self-signed certificate. This is one created by the developer themselves. Think of this as similar to creating a wax seal in the shape of your signature. If you were to seal something and apply a wax seal, anyone else could compare that item and another you seal to verify that the two were, in fact, sealed by the same individual. No third-party has verified who you are, or that the signature within the seal belongs to you. If someone looks at two (or more) things that you have sealed (or signed, getting back to the digital signature side of things), they can tell that the same person sealed both of them; they cannot, however, tell with any degree of confidence the identity of that person.

Android apps must be signed before they can be installed on a device. The Android system, however, does not require the certificate used to sign the app to be issued by a CA and will happily accept self-signed certificates (indeed, self-signed certificates are the standard way of signing Android apps). The Android toolset and development environment supports both debug keys/certificates and release keys/certificates. When you are developing and testing your app, whenever you compile, the toolset will sign the resulting APK (Android package) file with an automatically generated key. Indeed, you may not even realize that this APK signing step is happening, as there is no indication in the standard compile/build process that even alludes to it. This will work fine while testing your app on the Android emulator and will enable you to install your app on actual devices to test, but before you can deploy your app to the Android Market, you will need to generate an APK with a release key/certificate.

Release signing is somewhat different. If you are using the Eclipse ADT Plugin, you need to export your app using the Export wizard. If you are using command-line tools, you need to compile your app to an unsigned APK and then manually sign that APK using the *jarsigner* tool included with the Development Tools package. If you do not already have a self-signed certificate with an associated private key, you can generate one using the Eclipse plugin or using the *keytool* on the command line.

The exact steps that you will need to go through to generate a self-signed certificate and the associated private key can be completed using either the Eclipse ADT Plugin or the command-line tools installed as part of the Android Development Tools. If you need specific directions on how to complete this process using the tools, check the Android developer site (*http://developer.android.com*) and look for the App Signing topic (*http://developer.android.com/guide/publishing/app-signing.html*).

Once you have your private key in place, you need to protect it. Remember that anyone who gains access to your private key can sign apps, making them appear to have been created by you. When you create your private keys, put them into a keystore. Think of this as a big safe that protects your keys. The primary lines of defense here are the passwords that protect the private key, of which there are two. You need to specify a password to open that keystore and access the keys. Make this a strong password. The same goes for the password that protects the private key itself, as you can set passwords on both the keystore and the individual keys. Do not share your password or keys with anyone else. Your private key can let anyone else identify as you, so protect it!

Protection and Recovery

There is an important caveat here: while you need to protect your private keys, you also need to make sure that you retain access to them. If you protect your key by having only one copy of it with very restricted access, and the drive containing that key were to die, for example, you would never be able to sign anything with that key (which is tied to your identity as a developer) ever again. Creating a backup in some geographically and logically distinct location is vital, and the security of this backup location is critical as well. Protect the key, but make sure you have a secured backup copy as well. In addition, you may want to let a trusted person know how to access the key should you be away or incapacitated, to ensure the continued ability of your development to occur.

With an appropriate digital certificate and associated private key, you can sign your apps and release them. What does this actually mean? Well, the certificate identifies the developer, and a string with your information is shown on the device that the app is installed on. Apps that are signed by the same developer (using the same private key) are also afforded the ability to interact with each other at a higher degree than nonrelated apps, as we have already seen. Updates to existing applications must also be signed with the same key. Remember, when you sign an app using your private key, you are putting your stamp and identity on the app. This is why you need to protect that key: your reputation as a developer, and the protections built into the Android system to protect your app from others, are dependent on it.

Process Design

As we have discussed, Android UIDs are created and assigned on a per-package basis. It is possible to configure your apps so that more than one app shares the same UID, enabling the apps to share data and resources. To do so, you would modify the *AndroidManifest.xml* file for each app, in the group that you want to share the UID, so it includes a `sharedUserId` attribute in the `<manifest>` tag. All applications with the same tag value will share the same UID, and therefore be treated by the Linux kernel as the same app and have the same access to other apps' data. The value of the `sharedUserId` attribute is a string and needs to be common to all packages that will run under the same UID. In order to avoid conflicts, you should choose a string that is highly unlikely to match any that another developer would use, so it is suggested you create something within a namespace you control. For example:

```
<manifest xmlns:android="http://schemas.android.com/apk/res/android"
  package="com.example.test.sillyprogram1"
  android:sharedUserId="com.example.test.sharedUID" >
  .
  .
  .
</manifest>
```

If this tag is included in two applications, they will run as the same UID on the device and have access to each other's data. You can also programmatically determine the `sharedUserId` that a package runs under.

```
import android.content.pm.PackageManager;
import android.content.pm.PackageInfo;

PackageInfo pi = getPackageManager().getPackageInfo("com.example.test", 0);
System.out.println("The specified sharedUserId is: " + pi.sharedUsedId);
```

There are some limitations to this shared UID capability. All packages that use the same `<sharedUserId>` attribute must be signed by the same digital certificate (meaning that they are released by the same developer). Any package that specifies a `sharedUserId` can be installed on a device if the specified string does not already exist; however, if that string has already been specified by another, already-installed application and that application is signed by a different certificate, installation of the new app will fail. We will discuss the signing of apps and digital certificates a little bit later on, but for now, note that each developer needs to sign his apps and that only apps that have the same developer can share UIDs.

Finally, let's address how components such as Activities, Services, etc., run in relation to the underlying Linux kernel. All components within a package normally run as part of the same process, whose name is based on the package attribute set in the `<manifest>` element for that package (`com.example.test.sillyprogram1` in the past example). However, each component that is part of the package can override that convention and run within its own, specified process (we will see how in just a little bit). This capability can be used for one of two purposes: to allow components that are part of different apps but written by the same developer to run in the same process, or to let components that are part of the same app to run in different processes.

In the first case, you can let multiple components that normally run in one process instead run in multiple processes. This can be done by specifying a process attribute in the component's entry in the AndroidManifest tag.

For example:

```
<activity
 .
 android:name="ActivityNumber1"
 android:process="com.example.text.processIDnumber1" >
 .
</activity>
<activity
 .
 android:name="ActivityNumber2"
 android:process="com.example.text.processIDnumber2" >
 .
</activity>
```

This will cause `ActivityNumber1` and `ActivityNumber2` to run as separate processes on the Android device.

It is also possible to specify that a component should run as its own, private to the application. To do so, simply specify the process attribute and begin the value with a colon. This will prevent any other component from sharing a process with the component. This also would result in such a component being able to crash without affecting other components. For example:

```
<activity
 .
 android:name="ActivityNumber66"
 android:process=":com.example.text.processIDnumber66" >
 .
</activity>
```

In the second case, you can let components from different packages run in the same process. To do this, the specified components must be created by the same developer, and therefore signed by the same digital certificate. In addition, the components must specify the same `sharedUsedId` attribute. Finally, the name specified to the process attribute must begin with a lowercase letter; this causes the Android system to make the process name global so that other components will be able to utilize it when they start up. For example:

```
<activity
 .
 android:name="ActivityNumber40"
 android:process="com.example.text.sharedProcessIDnumber" >
 .
</activity>
```

This will cause `ActivityNumber40` to run in the same process as every other Application, Activity, and Service that specifies `com.example.test.sharedProcessIDnumber` as its process attribute.

The process attribute can be applied to multiple components within <manifest>: Application, Activity, and Service. All components of an Application use the specified process unless they override it with a process attribute of their own. In the case of an Activity or Service, specifying a process attribute will override any similar process attribute specified in the containing Application tag. This is a form of more granular control of the process that a component runs in.

Android Filesystem Isolation

As we have seen, Android does a good job of isolating apps from one another. Each app runs in its own Linux process with its own UID by default. Only apps that are created by the same developer and signed with the same digital certificates can weaken this isolation and to do so requires explicit configuration. While this design prevents apps from sharing memory and reading or writing data used by other apps, the standard Linux-based architecture extends further to other portions of Android, as we shall see.

The standard way that Android lays out the filesystem on a device is to create an app-specific directory under the path */data/data/app_package_name*. This directory is configured such that the associated app's UID is the owner and only the owner permissions are set; no other UIDs have access to it because no group or global permissions are configured. Within this directory is */files*, where all files created by the app are installed and created. By default, when new files are created, permissions are set to give the app's UID full control (as it is the owner of the file) and no other permissions are set, thus isolating access to the file from any other apps.

There are four important caveats to this setup:

- Because file isolation is based on UIDs, apps that are configured to run with the same UIDs can access each other's files.

  This exception arises by design, as apps can run with the same UID only if they are configured that way. As a developer, you should configure your apps to run with the same UID only if they need to communicate using shared resources for legitimate needs. Because that shared UID will have full control of the file, any app that uses it will be able to do whatever it wants with it.

- A user who accesses the Linux kernel using the root UID will be able to bypass any permissions on any file, allowing access to any data stored by any app.

  This exception exists because Android-based devices can be rooted, and is the same for any Linux-based system, or any that has the concept of a superuser account. If the data your app is storing is sensitive enough that you care about a user with root privileges accessing it outside of your app, employ extra methods such as encryption to protect it. These techniques will be discussed fully in Chapter 5.

- Any data written to external storage, such as SD cards, lacks Linux permission-based access control. Thus, any file written to external storage is accessible by any app on the device (or off the device and capable of accessing the storage media).

This exception exists because Android devices typically use SD-based external media and these media devices are formatted using a filesystem that does not support standard Linux-based permissions. If your app writes to external media and you need to ensure that other apps do not access that data, you need to use techniques such as encrypting that data.

- As the developer, you can specify different permissions on files.

  This is not really an exception, but simply a developer choice to alter the default case and make certain resources available to other apps. Details follow.

As discussed earlier, Android sets Linux permissions for all files created by an app with full control for the owner (the app's UID) and nothing else. When you create a file, you can modify that default by supplying one or more of the filesystem permission flags to the openFileOutput() method call.

MODE_PRIVATE
This is the default, granting full control to the app's UID and nothing else.

MODE_WORLD_WRITABLE
Allows all apps on the device to write to this file.

MODE_WORLD_READABLE
Allows all apps on the device to read this file.

These flags work by logically ORing them together, so the following method call would create a file named *scores* with both global read and write permissions:

```
OutputStreamWriter out = new OutputStreamWriter(
        openFileOutput("scores", MODE_WORLD_READABLE | MODE_WORLD_WRITEABLE));
```

The general rule of thumb is to assign app resources such as files, in this case, just enough permissions to do what needs to be done and no more. In information security terms, this is known as the Principle of Least Privilege. If your app does not need to share data with any other apps, use the default configuration and do not allow any such access. If you need to share data with one other app, and it is your app, you may want to use a shared UID approach, as this will share the data with just that one other app. If you are storing data that you want to make available to the entire device—and let's hope it is not sensitive data—you may want to apply the world permission flags. It's all about what you need to share, and making sure that whatever you decide is appropriate, based on a risk analysis.

Android Preferences and Database Isolation

Two others ways that Android apps store data, in addition to files, are SharedPreferences and databases. SharedPreferences is a basic framework that allows your app to store name/value pairs (primitive data types only) for easy access; this construct exists for configuration data and other similar purposes. Android also includes a SQLite implementation that allows apps to create and manage databases for storage of structured data more complex than you can do with name/value pairs or flat files. Both constructs have isolation mechanisms based on underlying Linux permissions, very similar to files.

SharedPreferences are accessed using SharedPreferences objects within a running app and as XML files on the filesystem. They are written to the filesystem under a /shared_prefs directory within the app's /data/data/app_package_name directory. SharedPreferences are created using the getSharedPreferences() method, which takes the same flags as openFileOutput() does, allowing you to specify that these stored preferences can be world readable or writable. Again, the default is to keep the preferences private, with only the app's UID allowed access, and the Principle of Least Privilege tells us that this is a good way to leave things unless you explicitly need to do otherwise.

For relational databases, SQLite is available within the Android system. Databases are created using the openOrCreateDatabase() method, which accepts the same permission operating modes as openFileOutput() and getSharedPreferences() (note that there are multiple methods with this name and the other version does not support these permission operating modes; make sure you are calling the correct method). Databases are created in the /databases directory under the app's /data/data/app_package_name directory and, by default, are accessible only by the UID of the creating app. For example, to create a database named Contacts and make it private to the creating app:

```
SQLiteDatabase myContactDB = openOrCreateDatabase(
        "Contacts", MODE_PRIVATE, null);
```

To create the same database and make it readable but not writable to every other app on the device:

```
SQLiteDatabase myContactDB = openOrCreateDatabase(
        "Contacts", MODE_WORLD_READABLE, null);
```

This would have the effect of allowing any other app to read the Contacts database, but only the creating app would be allowed to write to it (as it is still the owner and the owner has full control). Remember the Principle of Least Privilege: if others app may need to consume the data, but only this one should produce it, only read permissions are necessary.

From a design perspective, note that in the model assumed here (one app creates a database that others consume), a world-readable SQLite database is probably not a good choice; a Content Provider would most likely be more appropriate. Also, note that an alternate (and preferred) method of creating a database is to use a SQLiteOpen Helper. This always creates the database with MODE_PRIVATE permissions, so if you really want to create a database with different permissions, you will need to use the openOr CreateDatabase() method.

Moving up the Layers to System API and Component Permissions

As we have seen, much of the separation between apps on an Android device rests with the underlying Linux kernel. By default, each app runs with its own UID and the kernel prevents apps from accessing memory of other apps by default. Persistent resources created by apps such as files, stored user preferences, and databases have a similar permission model applied, where Linux permissions are set at the filesystem level to make sure that only the creating app can access the resource. We have also seen two coarse-grained access control mechanisms: a technique that allows apps created by the same developer to run as the same UID and bypass this isolation, and the ability to make persistent resources accessible by other apps on the device. This model is provided by the underlying Linux kernel and is central to the security model of the Android system.

At a higher level, Android introduces the concept of *app permissions*. Under this system, developers (including those at Google who develop the system APIs) create a formal permission that serves two purposes: apps can request the permission and the code can check to see if a running app has been granted that permission. For example, the Android system has a permission defined as INTERNET. When any app tries to access the networking system and open a socket, the networking APIs check to make sure that the calling app has been granted this permission. If it has, the call proceeds. If it has not, the call will fail in some way (most of the time, a `SecurityException` will be thrown, but this is not guaranteed). Chapter 3 discusses the Android permission model and how to use it.

CHAPTER 3

Application Permissions

As we discussed in Chapter 2, Android takes a different approach to running apps than traditional, desktop-based systems. On traditional systems, apps run under the account of the user who started them, and run with whatever permissions were granted to that user account. There are no per-app separation mechanisms. In addition, all apps running under that same user account have the same level of access to system APIs and other services provided by the underlying environment; both a document viewer and a VoIP application have the same level of access to the networking system because they run under the same UID by default. If a user has full root access to a system, any app that user started will run with full access to the system, and all the data on it, by default. This is the fundamental assumption of this traditional security model: all apps running on behalf of a user should be granted the same privileges and permissions.

In the Android model, each app runs as its own user account. This has the effect of separating the apps and ensuring that they can access only their own data, not data belonging to other apps, by default. Android then goes further and applies a comprehensive permissions system to services that are provided for use of installed apps. In order to make use of services provided by other code on an Android device that may be sensitive or dangerous, such as accessing a user's personal data or opening an Internet connection, an app must first request and be granted permission by the device's user. Android uses an install-time permission request model, where an app specifies which of these permissions it requires in its manifest. Before the app can be installed, the user must review the list of potentially dangerous things that the app is requesting to be allowed to do and approve them before installation is allowed to continue. This has the effect of informing the user what things the app would be able to do if installed and allows the user to make an informed decision about whether those permissions make sense before granting them.

This model provides two primary benefits over more traditional ones.

First, it allows the user to see, before an app is installed, all of the dangerous things that the app could do. Apps must specify which of these dangerous actions they may do in their manifest or attempts to perform them will fail, as the apps will lack permission to do them. A user downloading a game that runs entirely locally will see that the game is requesting permission to access SMS messages, make phones calls, and obtain full Internet access, which does not make any sense, and will choose not to install the game. This type of knowledge is not available to a user installing a similar game on a traditional desktop computer system; it doesn't have to enumerate the dangerous actions it could perform and tell the user in advance.

Second, this permissions model allows containment of an attack on a legitimate app. Apps inevitably contain coding problems and in many cases, errors in apps allow skilled attackers to take over the running app and cause their own arbitrary code to run in the same context as the compromised app (with the same UID and the same permissions). In a traditional system, if a web browser's scripting engine was compromised by an attacker, the attacker's code would run with the full privileges of the browser, which are equal to the full privileges of the user that started the browser. On an Android device, a compromised web browser would run the attacker's code with the full privileges of the compromised app and would therefore be limited to the permissions that the app has declared and been granted. But the browser may not have requested permission to touch any of the user's personal data (or it might have...what are the pros and cons of having a browser being able to access all of your personal data, and what does a risk analysis of allowing it to do so reveal?) and therefore the attacker would not be able to use such a compromise to extract that data.

A legitimate question that naturally arises, once one understands this permissions model, is, "Do users really read the permissions requested by a new app and make an informed decision about installing or not installing an app?" Basically, will users just approve any permissions set for an app they want to use (or even just try) or do they actually care about what is included in the list they agree to? This is a valid question, as the permissions model is effective only if this actually happens. Fundamentally, there is no way to force a user to truly understand what they are agreeing to, which is why descriptions for permissions are usually kept short and easily understandable. It truly is up to a user, using her own judgement, to scrutinize the permissions list for a new app. Some users will approve anything to play a game they want to try and some users will think long and hard about granting an app any dangerous permissions. Developers have a key role in this process, too. If users are always presented with a long list of dangerous permissions for every app they install, they will fatigue of reviewing them and keep approving them. If, however, the amount of permissions requested by apps is kept low, users will be more likely to scrutinize those that are presented to them. By minimizing the amount (and type) of permissions your app requests, you contribute to the overall security of the platform (for this and multiple other reasons, which we will explore in this chapter).

It is interesting to note, and keep in mind, that sometimes the motivation behind a permission request may not be obvious. For example, in Android 1.5 and before, all applications had access to external storage (such as an SD card). So, if an application targets version 1.5 of the platform or before, that application will always request the

WRITE_EXTERNAL_STORAGE permission, even if the application has no intention of ever accessing that storage.

So that is why the Android permissions model is designed the way it is. This is a modern approach, seen most prominently in Android right now, to address the reality that the fundamental tenant still driving desktop security models today—that all apps running on behalf of a user should be granted the same privileges and permissions—is no longer a valid way to design a security model. By implementing this app-specific, permissions-based model, Android provides the two primary benefits of allowing a user to know every dangerous action an app might perform and mitigating the consequences of an app being compromised by an attacker. Now that the design principles of the model are understood, let's move on to how it is implemented in Android.

Also, keep in mind that Android is the only current mobile platform with this type of permission system built-in and required for applications. The ability to restrict an application's behaviors and capabilities is a significant and powerful capability that other major platforms do not offer. This is both a great strength for the Android platform and a great opportunity for you, as a developer, to create more secure applications.

 Some current malware that target Android devices attempts to trick the user into installing them and granting a large set of permissions. A frequent technique of attackers is to make a malicious application look like an innocent one that the user would want to install. Another common technique is to reissue a legitimate application with an "added on" module, so that a user downloading a legit application from a nontrusted source would acquire that application with some malware riding along...with the same permissions granted to the application. So, once again, be careful!

Android Permission Basics

The Android permission model is based on the central construct of a *permission*. A permission is something that is granted to apps and required by APIs (or certain functions within code) in order to run. A simple example is the Android INTERNET permission; all of the networking APIs require a calling app to have this permission in order to execute the requested action of allowing network communications. Opening an outgoing network connection is something that not all apps need to do, and an activity that could cause the user to incur additional charges if they pay for the amount of data their device sends or receives (plus, this is the typical way an app would send sensitive data off the device to be exploited). So, opening a network connection is restricted by the INTERNET permission.

Android apps request permissions when they are installed. As a developer, you are responsible for determining which permissions your app requires and specifying all of these permissions in the *AndroidManifest.xml* file. For example, if your app wanted to communicate over the network, it would need to have an entry like this in its manifest:

```
<manifest xmlns:android="http://schemas.android.com/apk/res/android"
package="com.example.testapps.test1">
    ...
    <uses-permission android:name="android.permission.INTERNET" />
    ...
</manifest>
```

In this case, INTERNET is a permission created and used by the standard Android libraries. Your app, by specifying it, is saying that it will use the networking libraries at some point. The qualified name (beginning with `android.permission`) is how the Android system knows that an Android system permission is the one you are saying the app uses. There are a great number of system permissions within Android, and they are all specified as static String members of the `android.Manifest.permission` class. Because of this, along with the decision to locate the lines just shown in the app's manifest, Android permissions are sometimes called Manifest permissions. This also differentiates them from the Linux permissions discussed in Chapter 2. System permissions will be further discussed later on in this chapter.

While the Android system specifies a great number of system permissions that are required to access certain portions of the default APIs, there is nothing to prevent an app from using custom permissions, where the app defines a new permission and then runs with that permission, provides an API (or methods) that require a calling process to have that permission, or both. The permissions system is a powerful construct that is meant to be used and extended by app developers outside the core Android developers.

We have seen that an app needs to specify which permissions it requires in its manifest. The question then remains: how are these permissions granted? This is all handled when the app is installed. At that time, its *AndroidManifest.xml* file is read and the list of all permissions it needs to run is parsed. The installer then generates a list of these permissions (not all of them, as we will see in a bit) and prompts the user to review and approve them. This is an all-or-nothing process; either the user can choose to accept the list of permissions that the app claims it needs and the app will then install, or the user can choose to reject the list and the app's install will fail. Once an app is installed, no further interaction with the user will take place to let them know that a certain permission is being exercised or to confirm that the user still wants to allow the app to execute an action requiring a permission check. This design choice, to confirm each app's permissions with the user only at install time, is a key design decision for Android's permission model.

Now is a good time to think about how and where permissions are enforced. If you are writing an app that only calls other APIs and services, you need to determine which permissions are required by the APIs and services your app calls, and specify them in your manifest. You are the consumer of such services and need to ask permission. We will discuss this process in great detail in just a little bit. If, however, you are including methods that other apps will call, or other types of interprocess communication endpoints, you are sitting on the other side of the table as a provider of services; you are the one who needs to grant permission. Thus, you'll need to include code in your app that checks to make sure that whichever app is calling you has the correct permissions. This is a somewhat more complex matter, so let's explore the simpler permission-consumer app model first.

Using Restricted System APIs and the User Experience

As mentioned before, when an app is strictly a consumer of data and does not provide a mechanism for other apps to interact directly with it, such as providing callable methods or accessible ContentProviders, developer interaction with the Android permission system is largely limited to making sure that the permissions required for the APIs and other system mechanisms that the app consumes are listed in the *Android-Manifest.xml* file. The default set of Android permissions are grouped into four main categories:

Normal
> Permissions in this category cannot impart real harm to the user. For example, the permission to change the device's background wallpaper falls into the Normal category. Normal permissions are granted to a requesting app by default upon installation and the user does not need to explicitly confirm them. However, the user has the option to check these permissions upon installation and can review them at any time.

Dangerous
> Permissions in this category can impart harm to the user, by accessing private data (such as contacts), or making outgoing network connections. Dangerous permissions are explicitly shown to the user before an app is installed and the user must choose to grant the permissions or not, determining whether the installation continues or fails, respectively.

Signature
> This category of permissions is automatically granted to a requesting app if that app is signed by the same digital certificate as the app that declared/created the permission. In the case of default/system permissions, as this code is signed by the device manufacturer, requesting apps not created by the manufacturer will always be denied a Signature-level permission. This type of permission is intended for one app developer to share data between two or more of their apps (but not apps written by other developers) without burdening the user with the need to confirm that ability. The user is not prompted upon installing an app that requests Signature permissions: if the app is signed by the same certificate as the declaring app, the permission will be automatically granted; if not, the app being installed will not be granted the permission.

SignatureOrSystem

> Permissions in this category follow the same rule as Signature permissions, except that they are automatically granted to the Android system image in addition to requesting apps signed with the same certificate. This type of permission is used by device manufacturers to allow applications created by different vendors to work seamlessly together within that manufacturer's Android builds. The use of this type of permission is generally discouraged, and developers writing apps for distribution through traditional mechanisms such as the Android Market should have no need to ever create permissions of this type.

With these categories of permissions available, developers are expected to include a permission check in any API that fits the criteria specified above. If an action is sufficiently risky so that any random app should not be performing it, it should require an appropriate permission. For example, one of the Normal category permissions is SET_WALLPAPER. Changing the device's background wallpaper will not result in any sensitive information being sent off the device or the user incurring any additional charges for network or other message access. However, the user is likely to be annoyed or inconvenienced by such action if an app changes the wallpaper when it should not be. So the ability to do so is restricted by a permissions check. Opening an outgoing network connection, as we've seen, is at quite a different security level, so the INTER-NET permission is in the Dangerous category. Along similar lines, the ability to read or send SMS messages is also protected by Dangerous permissions. In fact, there are separate READ and WRITE permissions for SMS messages—remember the Principle of Least Privilege and request only the permissions needed by your app.

Since developers put permission checks on sensitive APIs and other methods of interacting with other apps (such as subscribing or querying ContentProviders), it is imperative that you determine which of these protected accesses your app will take advantage of, and declare the permissions in your manifest. As we have mentioned before, a common way for a protected API to fail if you try to access it without sufficient privileges is to throw a SecurityException. However, this is not guaranteed to happen, and how a failed permissions check should expose that information to the calling app is not directly specified or enforced. Therefore, the burden rests on you, as the developer of the calling app, to determine which permissions are necessary.

Unfortunately, this is not always a straightforward task. The Android APIs, and other interaction mechanisms, are documented online, and many of the methods that require a permission to successfully execute document that fact. However, not all do. Indeed, as each API is responsible for making its own permission checks, and each API developer is responsible for his own documentation, the API documentation is not 100% complete with regard to permissions required. Indeed, Internet message boards and other methods of developer communications are often filled with questions as to which permissions certain APIs require and so on. Now, this is not to say that you are entirely on your own. The API documentation, although it does contain oversights and omissions, is a great place to start, and many developers have most likely worked through the same permissions-related problems that you may be facing and are willing to share such information. However, it is still your burden to determine which permissions your app requires and to include those permissions in your manifest. Also, keep in mind that permissions may be required for other interactions besides API method calls. For instance, ContentProviders may require specific permissions for query, insert, update, and delete operations, and Intents may require certain permissions to be either called or created.

So, there may be work involved to make sure your app will not fail because you have failed to include the permissions it requires in its manifest file. However, the opposite problem also exists and is just as bad. You do not want to include more permissions in your manifest than you actually need. This issue goes to the heart of the Android permission model. The model exists so that apps run only with the permissions they actually need to do their job (Principle of Least Privilege). If your app includes permissions in its manifest that it does not actually need, you are violating that model. That can have two major repercussions, both of which parallel the two primary benefits of the permission model that we already discussed.

First, the permissions model exists to allow users to have accurate information about which sensitive activities an app may perform, so that they may make an informed decision on whether they want to allow the app to install and run. Your inclusion of permissions in the manifest is an explicit statement to the user that your app will use these permissions and the user is basing their decision on your claim. One of the most significant issues with this point is more user acceptance driven than security driven. The more permissions your app requests, the more likely a user (especially a security-conscious one) is to reject it at installation time. If you include the INTERNET permission in your local-only game, for example, a user may legitimately wonder why such an app would request that permission and refuse to install it, which is a perfectly sensible action (and one of the key behaviors the model hopes to encourage!). Because you presumably want as many users as possible to install your app, you should ask for just the permissions you need and no more. Moreover, minimizing the permissions your app requests may contribute to a more secure Android culture, where users take the time to examine all permission requests. So it is to everybody's advantage to use as few of the dangerous permissions as possible.

Second, the permissions model provides some mitigation against exploitation of vulnerabilities in your app. Suppose you release your app and then find you included an error in your network processing that allows an attacker to send some packets to your app and then gain control over it, forcing your app to execute any instructions the attacker wants it to. This is a frightening (although all too common) scenario, but the permissions model can reduce the amount of damage that attacker can do. Suppose that the attacker wants to download all of your contact information to target other users with. If you did not specify the READ_CONTACTS permission for your app, the attacker cannot use a compromise of your app to do so, as the process it is running under does not have permission to access the contacts list. This is the real beauty of the permissions system and why the Principle of Least Privilege is so important; mitigating the consequences of a successful attack is a wonderful thing.

Another aspect of your development lifecycle that may be affected by the permissions model has to do with automatic updates. In modern versions of Android, apps can be set up to automatically update through the Android Market, allowing you to get the most recent version of your app to your users very quickly and efficiently. However, automatic updating works only if the update does not include any additional permission requests. For example, if your app did not require Internet access (the INTERNET permission) but you then release an update that does use that permission, the app will not automatically update and users will just see a message that an update is available instead. Only after they are presented with the new permissions and agree to grant them will the new version be installed. This functionality exists to prevent app developers from specifying one set of permissions, which users agree to grant, and then grabbing more without the user knowing about it, which would violate the Android permissions model.

If you do not provide services for other apps to use, be that by API calls, ContentProvider interactions, Activity-invoking Intents, or so on, your involvement with the Android permissions system is pretty straightforward and is limited to the set of lines I showed before for the *AndroidManifest.xml* file. We'll turn next to programs that create permissions.

Custom Permissions

As we have discussed, you will need to create a custom permission if you are writing an app that will provide some service to others apps and you want to restrict which apps can access it. The first step to doing this is to actually declare the permission in the app that will be enforcing it. This is accomplished in the AndroidManifest.xml file:

```
<manifest xmlns:android="http://schemas.android.com/apk/res/android"
  package="com.example.testapps.test1">
    ...
    <permission android:name="com.example.testapps.test1.perm.READ_INCOMING_EMAIL"
            android:label= "Read incoming email"
        android:description="Allows the app to access the email retrieved
            from your email server using the test1 app. Any app you
            grant this permission to will be able to read all email
            processed by the test1 app."
        android:protectionLevel="dangerous"
        android:permissionGroup="android.permission-group.PERSONAL_INFO"
    />
    ...
</manifest>
```

This block of XML defines a new permission—READ_INCOMING_EMAIL—belonging to the `com.example.testapps.test1` package. This new permission has been given a name that should be self-explanatory. In this example, the test1 app is a basic app that implements an email client, separate from the Android client built in to the standard Android distribution. The label and description attributes of the permission declaration provide both a short and sweet summary of the permission and then a more detailed description, including the ramifications of granting the permission to another app. The two-sentence description follows a convention suggested in the Android documentation: the first sentence describes the permission and the second highlights what an app granted the permission would be allowed to do. From our description, it should be obvious to a user that if she grants this permission to another app, all email accessed using the test1 app may be exposed to that app.

The `protectionLevel` attribute is set to `Dangerous`, which is the appropriate type of permission based on the available options that we have seen before. Finally, the `permissionGroup` attribute is set. This is a label we apply to the permission that allows that Android package installer to organize the list of requested permissions when they are presented to the user upon app install. In this case, our new permission is of type PERSONAL_INFO, so it will be presented to the user right next to other permissions that allow access to personal information when the list is presented to the user. PERSONAL_INFO is defined in the `android.permission-group` package, which offers many options to choose from. You can also choose to define a new `permissionGroup` if you so choose. But because the goal is to organize the permission list given to the user as best as possible, it is good practice to use a predefined `permissionGroup`, so long as one does, in fact, apply to your new permission.

When you are defining permissions for your app, make sure that you create a model that applies the Principle of Least Privilege. Consider the permission that we have just declared. This permission is named READ_INCOMING_EMAIL, so we can assume that the only actions that our app will allow to a process granted this permission will involve reading email messages. If we wanted to allow other apps to write email messages or send them off the device, we would create separate permissions for those actions, each with a descriptive label and description. Other apps that want to make use of the email services we offer need to request these permissions separately, helping them request only the permissions they truly need. This is the proper application of least privilege concepts and results in a much better model than one that uses an all-encompassing permission for all access to email (like creating only one permission that provides full control to all of the email services we offer in our app).

Now that we have declared a new permission, apps can request it using the same `uses-permission` tag in the AndroidManifest.xml file as we used earlier for system permissions:

```
<manifest xmlns:android="http://schemas.android.com/apk/res/android"
 package="com.example.testapps.someotherapp">
 ...
    <uses-permission
 android:name="com.example.testapps.test1.perm.READ_INCOMING_EMAIL" />
 ...
</manifest>
```

This configuration will cause the someotherapp app to request the READ_INCOM-ING_EMAIL permission when it is installed. As we have declared this permission to be Dangerous, the install process will prompt the user to confirm she wants to grant this permission to someotherapp.

Now that we have declared a custom permission, and configured another app to request it, we need to modify our test1 app to make sure calling apps have been granted the permission. The most common way to do this is in a method call. For example, if our app has a method that we decide should be callable only by an app with the READ_IN-COMING_EMAIL permission, we could do so as follows:

```
int canProcess =
checkCallingPermission("com.example.testapps.test1.perm.READ_INCOMING_EMAIL");
    if (canProcess != PERMISSION_GRANTED)
        throw new SecurityException();
```

checkCallingPermission() is successful only if another process has called your method using some variety of Android interprocess communication (IPC), and only if that process was granted the permission you're checking. Note, then, that the call will always return PERMISSION_DENIED if you call it from a method in your own process. checkCallingPermission() is still the call you're most likely to include in your app because the primary reason you would be checking permissions is that you are exposing some methods to allow other apps to call them and you want to make sure that the calling app has the correct permissions. Think about the above example. Your app is checking for the READ_INCOMING_EMAIL permission, so it provides that ability to whatever app is calling it. In order to do so, your app must already be able to do this. In this scenario, you don't worry whether your own app can do what you coded it to do; you just want to make sure that whatever app called you has the READ_INCOM-ING_EMAIL permission before you proceed.

Another call can be used both by our own process and another calling process, to check whether it has a certain permission:

```
int canProcess =
checkCallingOrSelfPermission("com.example.testapps.test1.perm.READ_INCOMING_EMAIL");
    if (canProcess != PERMISSION_GRANTED)
        throw new SecurityException();
```

Here, checkCallingOrSelfPermission() returns PERMISSION_GRANTED to any caller with the specified permission, whether it's yourself or another calling process. As discussed previously, this type of check can be dangerous because a process without a certain permission could call your method, which runs as part of your process and therefore *does* have that permission, and gain access to a permission that it has not been granted. This is known as permission leaking and is a dangerous vulnerability in Android apps that deals with permission checking. My recommendation is that you should never call this method.

It is also possible to check whether a specific package has a specific permission:

```
    int canProcess = checkPermission(
        "com.example.testapps.test1.perm.READ_INCOMING_EMAIL",
        "com.example.testapps.someotherapp");
    if (canProcess != PERMISSION_GRANTED)
        throw new SecurityException();
```

Or to check whether a specific process with a specific UID has a specific permission:

```
    int canProcess = checkPermission(
        "com.example.testapps.test1.perm.READ_INCOMING_EMAIL", 3445, 312);
            // PID = 3445, UID = 312
    if (canProcess != PERMISSION_GRANTED)
        throw new SecurityException();
```

As you can see, there are plenty of different ways to check whether a specific permission has been granted. For practical considerations, you are going to need to check permissions if you offer up services to other apps and want to restrict which apps can take advantage of them. In the case of an API, where another app calls your app's methods, you will most likely want to take advantage of the checkCallingPermission() method above to ensure that the calling app has the specified permission. This will prevent an app that does not have that permission from calling your app, which does, and gaining that permission. Be careful about permission leakage and make sure you check the correct way.

 The programmatic way of checking for permissions that we have just discussed is very general and powerful, but it is not the preferred way of enforcing permissions. As we will see in Chapter 4, the best way to require specific permissions is to use declarative tags in the manifest entries for your application's components. This ensures that the proper permission checks are applied to all methods of the component and will make sure you do not miss a method or two, which can be common when using the programmatic approach.

That, in a nutshell, is how permissions work on Android. If you want to use custom permissions, you first need to create one. Then, you can programmatically check to see whether another app that is calling your code has been granted that permission. Now that we have explored the basics, we will move on to Chapter 4, which will discuss all of the different component types and how access to them can be restricted using custom permissions.

CHAPTER 4

Component Security and Permissions

The Types of Android Components

Android apps are composed of one of more components, of which there are multiple types. Each component can be secured in a slightly different way, so before we start talking about how to do so, a quick review of the types of components should be helpful.

The component that most Android developers learn about first is the Activity. An Activity is analogous to a single screen displayed on the device to a user that is composed of what the user actually sees. When building an app, you create classes that derive from the Activity base class and typically contain one or more Views, which are objects that users can interact with in some way, such as reading text displayed within the View, clicking a button, and so on. In proper application development terminology, the set of Activities is your application's *presentation layer*.

A Service is an Android component that is designed for background processing. These components can run when your app is not visible (that is, none of its Activities are being displayed to the user and are not active). Services typically either carry out some computations or update the data sources for your app. For example, if you were to build an email client app, a Service would run in the background to open up connections to the configured mail servers every so often, check for new mail, download it, and store new messages in the local database. Services can also be used to update Activities directly, to provide updates to the user directly via a Notification, or really for any other type of task that needs to occur in the background.

A Content Provider is a component designed to share data across apps. You can think of a Content Provider as the public interface to your databases, allowing other apps to connect and either run queries (retrieve data) or issue updates (store data). A Content Provider typically is used as a front end for a database created using the Android standard SQLite database system. As Content Providers are typically used to share data across apps, properly securing them so that appropriate apps can access specific data is critical; we will soon see how to accomplish this.

Content Providers are accessed using URIs of this form:

```
content://authority_name/path/id
```

The *authority_name* is specified when one declares a Content Provider in *Android-Manifest.xml*, and points to the Content Provider itself that will handle the reference (this is usually the full, all lowercase name of the implementing class). The *path* can be any number of segments, from zero on up, and is used by the Content Provider to find the data in question. In a basic implementation, the path would simply be the name of the table that the data is in. The *id* refers to a particular item, such as an email message stored by the Content Provider. Thus, a URI into a Content Provider used by an email client app to store messages may look like:

```
content://com.example.testapps.test1.mailprovider/messages/inbox/155
```

As we will see later, this URI-based method of addressing data within Content Providers is key to properly securing the data contained within.

A Broadcast Receiver is a type of component that listens for system messages called Intents. An Intent can be thought of as a request for a certain action to take place. Apps can create Intents and either send them directly to a specific component (usually an Activity or a Service) or broadcast them system-wide to all apps that are running. A Broadcast Receiver is a component that can receive these systemwide broadcasts and act upon them; it can choose to listen for all broadcast Intents or set up filters so that it receives only Intents for the specific actions it cares about (and would, presumably, take action upon). As with most broadcast systems, more than one Broadcast Receiver can receive, and act upon, a single Intent.

That, in a nutshell, is the selection of components that you can create to form an Android app. Some apps may be very simple, composed only of a few Activities. Some apps require background processing and will require a Service component, or components. Apps that store and maintain data may use Content Providers to make those databases accessible to other apps. Some apps may also choose to implement a Broadcast Receiver, if they want to perform certain actions in response to requests from other apps. Using this combination of components, apps ranging from the very simple to the very complex can be created. For each component, care should be taken to make sure that the component can be used as it is intended, and no more. Let us now turn to the ways that components can be locked down and secured.

Intercomponent Signaling Using Intents

Intents are the primary way for apps to send messages to other apps (and can also be used to send messages to other components within the same app). To send a message, an app creates an Intent object that signifies that it wants a certain action to take place. This Intent object can specify a specific Activity or Service that you want to start up, or it can specify a specific piece of data. In the later case, the Intent can either specify which components should perform an action on that piece of data, or just ask that someone should. This means that Android allows for Intents that have specific recipients (the Activity or Service that it wishes to interact with) as well as Intents that are broadcast throughout the system to any components that may be listening. We'll soon see how this can be controlled, and the relevant application security topics that arise.

One of the most common uses of Intents, and where most developers first encounter them, is having one Activity start another Activity. To do so, create an Intent with the name of the Activity you want to start and then pass that Intent to the calling Context to process. For example, for the current Activity to start up the `mainActivity` Activity, the following code could be used:

```
Intent actIntent = new Intent(myContext,
    com.example.testapps.test1.mainActivity.class);
myContext.startActivity(actIntent);
```

This code creates an Intent that specifies which Activity you want to start by providing its full class name. This is known as an *explicit* Intent. As we just discussed, you can create an Intent that does not specify which class should perform the desired action; this is known as an *implicit* Intent. In that case, the Intent is created with a specific action to be performed and most of the time, the piece of data that is to be acted upon. For example, if you want to display an image file, and you did not want to specify a specific app to do so, you would create and invoke the Intent like this:

```
Uri actURI = Uri.parse(pathToSpecificImageFile);
Intent actIntent = new Intent(Intent.ACTION_VIEW, actURI);
myContext.startActivity(actIntent);
```

When you issue this implicit Intent, the Android system will determine at run time which app should be invoked to handle the action specified in the Intent: the viewing of the image file located at the specific URI. The question then becomes: how does Android know which components should be used to perform a certain action specified in an Intent? The answer is the use of Intent *filters*. Each Activity, Service, and Broadcast Receiver can specify one or more of these filters, each of which specifies a type of action that they can process. For example, if we had an Activity with the ability to display GIF image files and wanted to expose that ability to other apps, we could set up an Intent filter on the Activity like this:

```
<intent-filter>
    <action android:name="android.intent.action.VIEW">
    <category android:name="android.intent.category.DEFAULT">
    <data android:mimeType="image/gif">
</intent-filter>
```

Note that in the case of an explicit Intent, where the component to receive the Intent is specified using its full class name, there is no checking of that component's Intent filters; an explicit Intent is always delivered to its specified component.

So far we have seen both explicit and implicit Intents. We can also use the Intent mechanism to broadcast messages to all apps that are listening for them. This broadcast Intent mechanism is used by the Android system itself to announce certain events that multiple apps may want to know about and respond to with some action. For example,

Android broadcasts an Intent when a telephone call is received on the device. This broadcast capability allows various components to share information in a very decoupled manner; when something that is of potential interest to multiple apps occurs, you can broadcast an announcement about it for anyone that is listening. As you can imagine, this is a powerful capability, and there are plenty of circumstances where you may want to control which components (of other apps on the device) can listen to your broadcasts, allowing them to be seen only by those apps that should have the rights to know about events. Let's review broadcast Intents briefly.

You may recall that we may use a Service in our email client app example to run in the background and constantly download new messages from configured mail servers. In the event that a message is downloaded, we may want to let the other portions of our app know about this so that the user can be notified. Indeed, it may be a good idea to let multiple components know about this event, so that each can take their own appropriate action in response to the new message's arrival. While the client's user interface, if active, may prepare to display the message, another app may make a copy of it, and so on. In this case, we will use a broadcast Intent to inform anyone that is listening about this event.

First, we need to declare a new action string, to define the action that is being announced within the broadcast Intent. In this case, we will call it MESSAGE_RECEIVED. To do so, we simply define a new String, like so:

```
public static final String MESSAGE_RECEIVED =
    "com.example.testapps.test1.action.MESSAGE_RECEIVED";
```

Then, to actually create the Intent and broadcast it throughout the Android system to all listening components, we issue:

```
Intent bdctIntent = new Intent(MESSAGE_RECEIVED);
myContext.sendBroadcast(bdctIntent);
```

Once we run this code, the device will broadcast the Intent out to any components that have intent-filters that allow them to receive it. To configure a component to receive these broadcast Intents, we would add a very basic intent-filter to our component in the manifest:

```
<intent-filter>
    <action android:name="com.example.testapps.test1.action.MESSAGE_RECEIVED">
</intent-filter>
```

Note that in this example, we do not include any information in the Intent, such as the URI of the new message. We simply broadcast the information that a message has been received; it is up to the components that receive the broadcast to take action on this notification. In order to receive broadcasts, an app should implement a Broadcast Receiver component, a type specifically designed to receive broadcast Intents and perform some action in response.

Now that we have discussed Intents as the primary communication path between components, both those within one app and those belonging to separate apps, we can move on to securing the various components that make up Android apps. In the course of this discussion, always keep in mind the Principle of Least Privilege, each component should be able to do exactly what it needs to do in order to carry out its function, and nothing else.

Public and Private Components

At the most fundamental level of access control lies the Android concept of *exporting*. Each component, be it an Activity, a Service, a Content Provider, or a Broadcast Receiver can be public or private. If a component is public, components of other apps can interact with it (start the Service, start the Activity, etc.). If a component is private, the only components that can interact with it are those from the same app or another app that runs with the same UID (see Chapter 3 for more detail).

The `exported` attribute in each component's declaration in the *AndroidManifest.xml* file determines whether the component is public or private. When `exported` is true, the component is public (and therefore exported to other apps), otherwise the component is private (not exported to other apps).

The default behavior depends on whether the component is likely to be used externally. In the case of Activities, Services, and Broadcast Receivers, the default depends on how the component is configured with regard to Intents. As we have seen, a component can specify an Intent filter that allows it to receive Intents from other apps to carry out tasks. As such, if a component specifies an Intent filter, it is assumed that you want the component to be accessed by other apps and it is, by default, exported and thus public. If, however, no Intent filter is specified for a component, the only way to send an Intent to it is to fully specify the component's class name. Therefore, it is assumed that you do not want to make this component publicly accessible, so the default `exported` is false and the component is private.

For example, a Service is normally public if an Intent filter is specified in its declaration and private if not. However, we may want to make a Service public but not specify an Intent filter, so that only components that know its full class name can make use of it (and we would probably want to restrict which components can access it using permissions, which we will discuss later). In this case, we need to specify the `exported` attribute as true, overriding the default:

```
<manifest xmlns:android="http://schemas.android.com/apk/res/android"
 package="com.example.testapps.test1">
 ...
    <service android:name=".MailListenerService"
             android:enabled="true"
             android:exported="true">
             <intent-filter></intent-filter>
    </service>
 ...
</manifest>
```

The default exported value for Content Providers is true. Because the primary purpose of a Content Provider is to share information between apps, it is assumed that these should be public and accessible by other apps.

Imposing Restrictions on Access to Components

Note that any component that is public (exported is set to true), can be accessed by any component in any app on the device. This global access is sometimes necessary: for example, the main Activity for an app is normally public and unrestricted so that the app can be started from anywhere. However, in many cases, components should be able to specify which components in other apps can access them. We will now go through the different types of components and discuss how to restrict access to them, so that the Principle of Least Privilege can be applied throughout a multi-component app.

Securing Activities

As we have discussed, Activities serve as the presentation layer for your app. Their security and permissions are pretty straightforward and just consists of who can start the Activity. To require a certain permission to start an Activity, you need to add the permission attribute to the specific Activity's entry in *AndroidManifest.xml*. For example, to declare an Activity that requires the START_ACTIVITY1 permission, the entry in the manifest would look like this:

```
<manifest xmlns:android="http://schemas.android.com/apk/res/android"
  package="com.example.testapps.test1">
  ...
    <activity android:name=".Activity1"

android:permission="com.example.testapps.test1.permission.START_ACTIVITY1">
              <intent-filter>
                ...
              </intent-filter>
    </activity>
  ...
</manifest>
```

If an app wanted to start this Activity, it would do so by creating an Intent specifying the desire to start the Activity and then call either Context.startActivity() or Activity.startActivityForResult(). If the caller has the specified permission (START_ACTIVITY1 in this case), both of these calls will succeed, resulting in the Activity being started. Without that permission, both will fail and throw a SecurityException.

Securing Services

Services are the background processing components in Android. It is possible to restrict who can interact with a service by applying permissions; this will affect any attempts to interact with the service by either creating it or binding to it. As Services typically perform some variety of processing that consists of updating databases, providing notifications of an external event, or performing some other task for the benefit of a component that will interact with the user, it is important to make sure that they are accessible only by appropriate consumers. To require a permission to create or bind to a service, simply add the permission attribute to the specific Service's entry in *Android-Manifest.xml*. For example, to declare a Service that requires the BIND_TO_MAIL_LISTENER permission, the entry in the manifest would look like this:

```
<manifest xmlns:android="http://schemas.android.com/apk/res/android"
  package="com.example.testapps.test1">
  ...
    <service android:name=".MailListenerService"
            android:permission=
                "com.example.testapps.test1.permission.BIND_TO_MAIL_LISTENER"
            android:enabled="true"
            android:exported="true">
            <intent-filter></intent-filter>
    </service>
  ...
</manifest>
```

Note that in this example, we create a service that does not have an Intent filter, so it can be invoked only by an Intent that fully specifies the class name. We did this to imply a design where only our own apps would connect to this Service and therefore would know the full name of our Service. As this service does not have an Intent filter, we also needed to specify the exported attribute as true, as this defaults to false for components that do not specify Intent filters.

If an app attempted to interact with this service—starting it by calling Context.start Service(), stopping it by calling Context.stopService(), or binding to it by calling Context.bindService()—the call would succeed if the caller has the specific permission (BIND_TO_MAIL_LISTENER). If the caller does not have this permission, the call would fail with a thrown SecurityException.

This capability controls who can interact with a service only at a very coarse level (you can control who can start, stop, and bind to a Service). You cannot restrict access permissions on a more fine-grain level using this mechanism, such as providing permission checks on specific callable methods of a bound service. For such flexibility, use the general capability of verifying permissions programmatically that we discussed in Chapter 3. You can call checkCallingPermission() to see whether the calling app has a specific permission at the entry point of any methods you think require permission checks over and above the permission configuration set for the overall Service. Of course, you can make such a check at any point in a method as well; doing so before performing a sensitive operation is the key.

Securing Content Providers

Content Providers are the standard way for apps to make their data available to other apps. As these components exist to share data among different consumers and suppliers, they raise the need for a more complex security model.

Unlike Activities and Services, Content Providers can specify two different required permissions: one for reading and one for writing. This allows apps to be configured using the Principle of Least Privilege and recognizes how common designs are where some apps should be able to read certain data, other apps should be able to write that data, and still others should not be allowed to access the data at all.

One common misconception about these permissions is that having the write permission automatically implies the read permission. The logic is that updating data (writing) is a more powerful permission than simply reading it and anyone that can write into a database should also be able to read from it. This is a fallacy, and the Android design, separating read and write permissions, acknowledges that. For example, consider an email client app (I really do seem to like this example when discussing component security, don't I?). In our app, we may implement a Content Provider to store email we download from a mail server. A Service may periodically connect to that mail server, download new messages, and put them into our database by writing to that Content Provider. The Service clearly needs the permission to write to the Content Provider, but does it need the permission to read from it? No. In fact, it should not have that permission, as it is not needed for it to do the job it performs. Remember the Principle of Least Privilege: grant the permissions needed to get the job done and no more.

For example, to declare a Content Provider that requires separate permissions to read or write data, the entry in the manifest would look like this:

```
<manifest xmlns:android="http://schemas.android.com/apk/res/android"
  package="com.example.testapps.test1">
  ...
    <provider android.name="com.example.testapps.test1.MailProvider"
            android.authorities="com.example.testapps.test1.mailprovider"
            android.readPermission="com.example.testapps.test1.permission.DB_READ"
          android.writePermission="com.example.testapps.test1.permission.DB_WRITE">
    </provider>
    ...
</manifest>
```

With Content Providers, permissions are first verified when you connect to the provider. When you do so, you can connect to it if you have either the read permission or the write permission. If you have neither, the connection request will fail with a thrown `SecurityException`.

Permissions are then checked when you attempt to interact with the Content Provider. Using its `query()` method requires the read permission, while using its `insert()`, `update()`, or `delete()` methods requires the write permission, as specified in the manifest declaration (`DB_READ` and `DB_WRITE` in this case). Again, note that having the write permission does not automatically give you the read permission; the two are separate and enforced independently. If you were to call one of these methods without the corresponding permission, the call would not succeed and a `SecurityException` would be thrown instead.

The ability to separate read and write permissions allows us to better control which apps can interact with our Content Providers and how they can do so. However, when permissions are enforced using these methods, they apply to all of the data within a given provider, which can sometimes be way too much. Let's think about our email client app again. We want to allow only the user interface components of our app to access the underlying Content Provider that holds all of the email; we certainly do not want arbitrary other apps to be able to do so, as email is sensitive information. However, what about the case of attachments to email? If an image or sound file is attached to a message, the email client app needs to be able to invoke the appropriate media handler to properly present that attachment to the user, and this would require the media handling app to have read permissions into the Content Provider that the attachment is stored in. This is clearly not a good idea, as we would be granting these apps the ability to read all of the stored email.

The solution to this problem is to make use of *URI permissions*. The Android designers have recognized that developers may need to grant permissions to certain portions of a Content Provider's database for a short period of time. The case of allowing a media app access to an attachment within the Content Provider when the user wants to display that attachment is an illustrative example of this (indeed, it is such a good example that it is the same one used in the Android documentation when it introduces URI permissions!). With this mechanism, any component that has permission to access a URI within a Content Provider can temporarily grant that access to another app/component. In the case of the email client app, the user interface app (which does have permission to the entire Content Provider with email and attachment content) could temporarily grant permission to the URI that contains an attachment to the image viewer that is being called upon to display the image, even though the image viewer has no permissions to access the Content Provider by itself.

In order to use the URI permission system, a Content Provider must be configured to allow this in the Android manifest. Because this system is used to extend permissions beyond what is normally configured, the mechanism is turned off by default. There are two ways to enable URI permissions: one that covers any URI contained within the Content Provider and another that covers only a subset of URIs. In order to enable temporary URI permissions globally within a Content Provider, set the `grantUriPermissions` attribute in the `<provider>` declaration to true, like this:

```
<manifest xmlns:android="http://schemas.android.com/apk/res/android"
  package="com.example.testapps.test1">
    ...
      <provider android.name="com.example.testapps.test1.MailProvider"
                android.authorities="com.example.testapps.test1.mailprovider"
                android.readPermission="com.example.testapps.test1.permission.DB_READ"
```

```
                    android.writePermission="com.example.testapps.test1.permission.DB_WRITE"
                    android:grantUriPermissions="true">
        </provider>
        ...
    </manifest>
```

Note that this configuration attribute does not actually grant those permissions simply by including this option; it merely allows a component that has the access already to temporarily grant those permissions later to another app.

This global configuration option allows the Content Provider to grant permissions to any accessible URI within it. It is entirely possible for a Content Provider to be interested only in granting temporary permissions to a subset of URIs. In our email client app example, we envisioned using this mechanism to temporarily grant media-handling apps access to attachments in our email database. It makes sense to store attachments in a different path within the database, separate from messages. For example, the URI to a mail message may look like this:

```
content://com.example.testapps.test1.mailprovider/messages/inbox/155
```

And the URI to an attachment may look like this:

```
content://com.example.testapps.test1.mailprovider/attachments/42
```

In this case, we may want to temporarily grant permissions to entries in the /attach-ments/ path, but never grant permissions to the /messages/ path. In this case, globally enabling URI permissions would violate the Principle of Least Privilege. In order to deal with this, we can omit the grantUriPermissions attribute and instead include separate <grantUriPermission> elements within the <provider> element. Each <grantUriPermission> element specifies a subset of the Content Provider for which it can grant URI permissions. For each such element, you include one of three possible attributes: path, pathPattern, or pathPrefix.

To specify a directory whose files can be accessed through URI permissions, use the path attribute in the <grant-uri-permission> element. For example, to allow URI permissions to be granted on the /attachments/ path, the relevant configuration would look like this:

```
    <manifest xmlns:android="http://schemas.android.com/apk/res/android"
        package="com.example.testapps.test1">
        ...
        <provider android.name="com.example.testapps.test1.MailProvider"
                android.authorities="com.example.testapps.test1.mailprovider"
                android.readPermission="com.example.testapps.test1.permission.DB_READ"
                android.writePermission="com.example.testapps.test1.permission.DB_WRITE">
            <grant-uri-permission android:path="/attachments/" />
        </provider>
        ...
    </manifest>
```

The path attribute is not recursive; if there is any subdirectory under /attachments/, no access is granted to files in that subdirectory. To specify a path that is a prefix (meaning that all URIs that fall under that path can be granted URI permissions), use the `path Prefix` attribute in the `<grant-uri-permission>` element. For example, if we wanted to be able to grant URI permissions on messages within our database (any path that began with /messages/), we could configure the Content Provider like this:

```
<manifest xmlns:android="http://schemas.android.com/apk/res/android"
  package="com.example.testapps.test1">
  ...
    <provider android.name="com.example.testapps.test1.MailProvider"
            android.authorities="com.example.testapps.test1.mailprovider"
            android.readPermission="com.example.testapps.test1.permission.DB_READ"
          android.writePermission="com.example.testapps.test1.permission.DB_WRITE">
        <grant-uri-permission android:pathPrefix="/messages/" />
    </provider>
  ...
</manifest>
```

Finally, the `pathPattern` attribute can be used to supply a full path just like the `path` attribute does, but supports wildcards. Wildcards in this type of specification follow the format of using an asterisk (*) to match zero or more occurrences of the character that immediately precedes it. So to match zero or more of the letter A, you would use the sequence `A*`. You can also use a period (`.`) to match any single character. To match zero or more characters (any characters), you would use the two-character `.*` sequence. For example, if you wanted to be able to grant permissions to any URIs that contain the string `public` in them, write:

```
<manifest xmlns:android="http://schemas.android.com/apk/res/android"
  package="com.example.testapps.test1">
  ...
    <provider android.name="com.example.testapps.test1.MailProvider"
            android.authorities="com.example.testapps.test1.mailprovider"
            android.readPermission="com.example.testapps.test1.permission.DB_READ"
          android.writePermission="com.example.testapps.test1.permission.DB_WRITE">
        <grant-uri-permission android:pathPattern=".*public.*" />
    </provider>
  ...
</manifest>
```

So we now see that Content Providers can be configured so apps that already have access to them can temporarily grant those permissions to other apps. Once the Content Provider has been configured in this way, the app needs to actually grant those permissions. This is fairly easy, as it consists solely of setting the appropriate flag in the Intent created to call the new app. To temporarily grant read permissions to the app being called, set the `FLAG_GRANT_READ_URI_PERMISSION` flag. To temporarily grant write permissions to the app being called, set the `FLAG_GRANT_WRITE_URI_PERMISSION` flag. In the case of our email client app, an Intent would be created that specifies the URI of the attachment that we want to open. Then the `FLAG_GRANT_READ_URI_PERMISSION` flag would be set on the Intent. When this Intent is passed to `Context.startActivity()`, the image viewer Activity would be started, targeting the URI within the Content Provider. Because the appropriate flag was set, the image viewer app would have permission to access the specific URI in the Content Provider and all would function as intended. For example:

```
Intent intent = new Intent(Intent.ACTION_VIEW);
intent.setFlags(Intent.FLAG_ACTIVITY_NEW_TASK);
intent.addFlags(Intent.FLAG_GRANT_READ_URI_PERMISSION);
intent.setDataAndType(uri, "image/gif");
startActivity(intent);
```

An alternative approach to specifying the flags in an Intent is to explicitly grant a specific app permissions on a Content Provider URI. Note that this is not the preferred way to pass permissions; the flags specified in the Intent is the standard approach. But to do the alternative approach in a program, you can use the `Context.grantUriPermission()` method, passing in the package name to which you wish to temporarily grant the permissions, the URI in question, and the Intent flags specifying which permission(s) you want to grant. For example, to grant another app read permissions to access a message within the email client's database:

```
uri = "content://com.example.testapps.test1.mailprovider/attachments/42";
Context.grantUriPermission("com.example.testapps.test2", uri,
    Intent.FLAG_GRANT_READ_URI_PERMISSION);
```

Of course, if you are going to grant another app permission into a Content Provider in this way, you need to revoke that permission when access is no longer necessary (remember, this is intended to be a temporary grant of permission). To do so, call the `Content.revokeUriPermission()` method, passing in the URI and the flags. Note that this method will revoke all permissions temporarily granted to that URI, along with permissions to any other URIs on the same path that had permissions granted this way. For example:

```
uri = "content://com.example.testapps.test1.mailprovider/attachments/42";
Context.revokeUriPermission(uri, Intent.FLAG_GRANT_READ_URI_PERMISSION);
```

This code will revoke granted permissions for /attachments/42. Had permissions been temporarily granted using this method to other items at the same path level, such as /attachments/22, those permissions would be revoked by this call as well.

Finally, it is also possible to programmatically check to see whether a specific app (if you know its process and UID) has been granted access to a specific Content Provider URI. Note that this mechanism only checks to see whether the specified process has been granted permission using one of the two mechanisms described in this section and does not consider broader, general access. Therefore you should rely on this approach only to check temporary URI permissions.

To check to see whether another app has the specific permissions, call `checkUriPermission()` and pass in the URI, the PID you want to check, the UID you want to check, and the flags you want to verify. For example:

```
int canProcess = checkUriPermission(uri, 377, 122,
Intent.FLAG_GRANT_READ_URI_PERMISSION);
if (canProcess != PERMISSION_DENIED)
```

```
{
    ...
}
else
    throw new SecurityException();
```

This code will check to see whether the process running with PID 377 and UID 122 has been granted read access to the URI specified. If you are handling an IPC for another app, you can use a different approach to check whether that calling app has been granted the specified permissions. Note that this method works only if you are processing an IPC from another app; if you are not, it will always return PERMISSION_DENIED:

```
int canProcess = checkCallingUriPermission(uri,
Intent.FLAG_GRANT_READ_URI_PERMISSION);
if (canProcess != PERMISSION_DENIED)
{
    ...
}
else
    throw new SecurityException();
```

And that's the word on Content Providers. These components require a longer discussion than the other components because they are the most tricky to secure. However, now that you understand the general concepts, it's not really that hard. Content Providers use standard Android permissions to allow apps read and/or write access to them. Many situations require more fine-grained access, so URI permissions are available for apps to temporarily grant permissions to certain content within a Content Provider when necessary. Once you understand how the URI permissions work, it is possible to grant specific apps the specific permissions they need to specific content at the specific times they need them. This is the Principle of Least Privilege at its finest.

Securing Broadcast Intents

As you will recall from our earlier discussion, messages are commonly broadcast out to any app that is listening for them using Broadcast Receivers. We discussed our email client app example and how the Service that is constantly checking for new mail may choose to send out a broadcast Intent when a new message has been received, so that multiple components may choose to act upon this. In this case, we most likely want to limit the components that can receive such a broadcast, as we do not want to go announcing to the whole world that an email message has just come in.

The sender of broadcasts can choose to apply an Android permission to each broadcast it sends, that broadcast will be delivered only to those Broadcast Receivers that both have an Intent filter that allows them to receive it and the specified permissions that indicate they are authorized to do so. In the case of our Service example, we can restrict which Broadcast Receivers are allowed to receive our broadcasts by sending the broadcast only to those with a MSG_NOTIFY_RECEIVE permission that we create for this purpose:

```
Intent bdctIntent = new Intent(MESSAGE_RECEIVED);
myContext.sendBroadcast(bdctIntent,
    "com.example.testapps.test1.permission.MSG_NOTIFY_RECEIVE");
```

Note that in many cases, when a permission check fails, a `SecurityException` is thrown. When we lock down broadcasts in this manner, no `SecurityException` will be thrown if a Broadcast Receiver specifies that they should receive these broadcasts but they do not have the specified permissions. Indeed, since this code attempts to send the specified broadcast Intent to any Broadcast Receiver with a matching Intent filter, some of these receivers may have the specified permission and some may not; no feedback is returned to the component sending the broadcast Intent as to which succeeded and which failed.

This mechanism enables the sender of a broadcast to specify which receivers are allowed to receive it. It is also possible to do the reverse: to configure a Broadcast Receiver to accept incoming broadcast Intents only from senders that hold the specified permissions. To do this, simply specify a permission attribute in the `<receiver>` element in AndroidManifest.xml. For example:

```
<manifest xmlns:android="http://schemas.android.com/apk/res/android"
  package="com.example.testapps.test1">
    ...
    <receiver android:name=".UIMailBroadcastReceiver"
            android:permission=
                "com.example.testapps.test1.permission.MSG_NOTIFY_SEND">
        <intent-filter>
            <action android:name="com.example.testapps.test1.action.MESSAGE_RECEIVED">
        </intent-filet>
    </receiver>
    ...
</manifest>
```

This declares a Broadcast Receiver that listens for `MESSAGE_RECEIVED` broadcast Intents and accepts them only from senders that have been granted the `MSG_NOTIFY_SEND` permission. If a `MESSAGE_RECEIVED` broadcast Intent arrives from a sender without that permission, it will not be delivered to this Broadcast Receiver.

It is also possible to register a Broadcast Receiver programmatically, instead of in the *AndroidManifest.xml* file, by calling `registerReceiver()`. In this case, you can still apply a permission restriction, only allowing senders with that permission to send to the registering Broadcast Receiver. For example:

```
IntentFilter intentFilter = new IntentFilter(MESSAGE_RECEIVED);
UIMailBroadcastReceiver rcv = new UIMailBroadcastReceiver();
myContext.registerReceiver(rcv, intentFilter,
    "com.example.testapps.test1.permission.MSG_NOTIFY_SEND", null);
```

As you can see, broadcasts can be secured in either direction. Senders of broadcasts can configure them so that only receivers with specific permissions are allowed to receive them. Receivers of broadcasts can be configured to accept them only from senders with specific permissions. Using a combination of these two mechanisms, it is possible to set up a broadcast architecture where each component that should be notified about certain events is notified (and those that should not be notified about them are not), and each component accepts event notifications only from authorized senders.

Putting It All Together: Securing Communications in a Multi-Tier App

The Android permission system allows the various components that make up an app to set restrictions on what other components can access them. While some basic apps are composed of just a few Activities, larger and more sophisticated apps are typically composed of a combination of Activities, Services, Content Providers, and Broadcast Receivers. In addition, Android encourages the use of decoupled components through the Intent system, where multiple components belonging to different apps can work together to fulfill a desired function. This method of app design, thinking in terms of components instead of apps, can result in many advantages, but can also result in many apps receiving access to data and information that they should not have. As such, a proper security architecture must be part of any involved app design. As a developer, you must consider what type of data and what type of service your components are providing and who should be granted access to them. Once you have determined that, the actual application of a permissions scheme to implement it is very straightforward.

For Activities, you need to carefully consider who should be able to invoke/start the Activity. For the initial Activity that will be displayed to the user when your app starts, no permissions are required. For other Activities, apply permissions so that the Activities in question can be started only by others that have the correct permissions.

For Services, you need to consider who should be able to start them, stop them, and bind to them. Because Services run in the background, it is likely they are providing some service that other components of your app will access. If they are doing anything with sensitive data or performing any functions that should not be available to any app in the world, permissions should be applied so that only apps that *should* have access to their functions are allowed. In addition, if your Service supports binding and allows apps to make calls to methods for functions it can provide, you may want to add further programmatic checks within some of those methods, if there are different levels of sensitivity. For example, in the email client app, a certain permission may be necessary to access a method that checks when the most recent email message was received, while a separate permission may be necessary to update the mail server settings. In such a case, restricting the different methods with different permissions is clearly necessary.

For Content Providers, careful consideration must be taken in designing their permissions. Read and write permissions can be set on Content Providers and any components that require access to the provider should be granted only the permissions that they truly need to perform their jobs. Content Providers also include the ability to grant URI permissions—whereby an authorized component may temporarily grant permissions to another component that does not have any rights itself—to specific pieces of data within the Content Provider. This allows a very fine-grain permission model to be set up and enforced, but requires careful planning. The `grant-uri-permission` configurations must be set up in the manifest. It is important to get these configurations right so that permissions cannot be temporarily granted to data that should never be accessed by components that do not carry the permissions specified for the Content Provider. It is strongly recommended that you use individual `grant-uri-permission` entries instead of the overall `grant-uri-permissions` attribute for the entire Content Provider, if the data within the provider can be segregated into sections that can be safely shared and those that cannot. Finally, once permissions are temporarily granted, they must be revoked once the necessary actions are carried out, so that permission is granted only during the time period it is needed for.

Broadcasts are a key technique for intercomponent communications. Mechanisms exist so that the senders of broadcasts can require any receivers that want to receive them to have certain permissions, and this should be enforced if the broadcast is at all sensitive. The opposite mechanism, allowing Broadcast Receivers to accept broadcasts only from those senders with specific permissions, allows receivers to accept messages only from those senders that they can trust (because they have been granted the permission). When using broadcasts to communicate information about anything sensitive, both mechanisms should be deployed, authorizing both receivers and senders, and barring unauthorized components from the system altogether.

Individually, each component type allows you to specify whom the component should be allowed to talk to. Put together, these mechanisms allow an Android app composed of multiple pieces to fully control how those pieces interact, both with other components of the same app and those that are part of different apps. Once the architecture of an app has been designed, applying the principles we have just discussed should be a fairly straightforward task and will result in communications that correctly employ the Principle of Least Privilege and a robust, rugged, more secure app.

CHAPTER 5

Protecting Stored Data

This chapter shows you how to protect data that your application stores on the Android device it runs on. This may include basic, nonsensitive data such as high scores on a game, or very sensitive data such as the user's bank account login details, should your app require access to such data. As you saw in Chapter 2, some of the built-in protections afforded your app by the basic architecture of Android should prevent other apps from accessing (or, potentially even worse, modifying) this stored data.

But basic access control, such as that provided by the operating system, is often not enough to protect against the risk of compromise (remember: if the risk, composed of vulnerability, threat, and consequences, is high, you must mitigate that risk down to a sufficiently reduced level). This is where cryptography comes into play; if data is stored in a scrambled or encrypted form, an attacker can get his hands on it without recovering the normal, unencrypted form. This is one of the primary advantages of cryptography, and what we will be discussing in this chapter.

The Threats and Vulnerabilities Against Stored Data

We have already seen, in Chapter 2s, how the Android system segregates data stored by apps from other apps. We have also seen how apps can share data amongst themselves and how we can use permissions and other access control mechanisms to specify what type of such accesses are allowed. All of these protections, offered to stored data or data at rest, rely on the mechanisms of the running Android system. They assume that the system is up and running as it should and that all accesses to stored data will be through these controlled channels. Unfortunately, this is just not always the case.

Vulnerabilities of Stored Data

All data that is stored on a typical Android device gets stored in some variety of mass storage device. Most devices include some storage internal to the device (included on the primary circuit board within the case) and a typically much larger amount of storage on a removable memory card. No special protections are afforded to data written by an app onto this storage, and accessing from a computer is quite straightforward (moreso with the memory card, which can simply be pulled out of a device and inserted into a computer, but getting at the memory internal to a device is not much more difficult). If your app stored some sensitive data, say bank account numbers or passwords for social media sites (going back to an example from Chapter 1), that data could be easily read by an attacker who happened to swipe someone's device, or even just its memory card. Offline access to the storage on an Android device is easy to obtain and affords an attacker full access to whatever your app stores.

In addition, as I have pointed out, any data stored on a memory card (usually an SD card) is not afforded any isolation by the underlying Linux kernel and can be freely accessed by any application while still in the device. This becomes a significant concern when you realize that not all developers understand this and store data on the media card without hesitation.

It is also possible (and not super difficult) to get root-level access to Android devices. As root is the superuser identity, anyone with root access can do anything they want to a system. In the case of Android, Google has made it easy for someone in possession of and access to (meaning they can unlock it) a device to gain root access to it. This allows complete and unrestricted access to the memory and storage while the device is running. The isolation provided to files, databases, and other resources simply does not exist when other apps can run with the root identity.

 The threat caused by root access to a device your application is running on goes beyond that of a user performing this action themselves. Some of the more advanced malware targeting Android devices make use of kernel-level vulnerabilities to obtain root themselves (and without evidence of this provided to the user). This allows the malicious code to run as root, able to bypass the Android security model. This is a prime example of where reliance on that model to protect sensitive data may not be sufficient.

Threats to, and Mitigations for, Stored Data

We have just talked about two vulnerabilities to data stored by your apps on Android devices. Thinking back to our previous risk discussion, we know that we also need to consider the threats to the data stored by our apps and the consequences if it were to be successfully attacked. For example, suppose you were to write a game that stored information such as high scores, player progress, and other such details. The risk of someone using a vulnerability in your code to read such data is probably pretty low, because there are no real consequences as this data is not sensitive. However, the risk of someone using such a vulnerability to modify such data, perhaps giving themselves a new high score or advancing past part of the game illicitly, may be a greater risk, especially if there are rewards offered for excellent play. What aspects of the risk equation change in this case?

Consider another example of the social media aggregator from our earlier discussion. Here, the risk of someone using a vulnerability to read stored data such as account passwords is probably pretty high, while the risk of someone modifying such data or deleting it is probably pretty low. What is the worst thing that someone could do if they could change the stored username and password an app uses for your Twitter access? The answer may make you consider this to be a higher risk than you may first think!

Remember, the steps you take to protect the data your app stores on the device must be appropriate given the threat. If your app stores no sensitive data, and the consequences of that data being either exposed to others, modified, or deleted is minimal, then you do not need to worry about things like applying proper permissions to your data store or encrypting your data. If, however, the data you are storing is very sensitive, and compromise of that data would lead to serious consequences, then you need to take more steps to protect it.

Protection Principles

Protection of stored data, or data at rest, is best accomplished using a series of protection mechanisms that reinforce each other. For example, if proper permissions are set on the data store your app is using, other apps will not be able to read or modify that data on a normally running Android system. We have seen that mechanisms do exist that would allow such compromises to occur. Sensitive data should also be encrypted, so that if an attacker is able to compromise the protections offered by the Android system and obtain access to the data, they cannot do anything with it. Deploying different layers like this is a common information security practice known as *Defense in Depth* (DiD).

We have also seen that the steps taken to protect stored data must be appropriate based on the risk of compromise. Along similar lines, before figuring out how to protect the data stored by your app, consider carefully what data you actually need to store. Do you really need to store bank account details? Do you need to store user account credentials? This goes back to the Principle of Least Privilege: apps should store the data needed to get their job done effectively and nothing more. If you don't store it, you don't have to worry about protecting it and there can be no compromise or repercussions!

 This is a very important point. Carefully consider what data your application needs to store to effectively accomplish its purpose. Store that data and nothing else. The less data you store, the less you need to protect.

What about the data that you do need to store? Modern cryptography has given us many tools and techniques that can be applied to protect stored data. In order to understand how we can protect data our apps store, we need to understand the basics of cryptography, and that is exactly what we will do in the next couple sections. After we do that, we will explore how we can use these tools to protect our data.

Cryptography Primer: Encryption

When people hear the word cryptography, they tend to think of encryption. Encryption, plain and simple, refers to the process of taking a message (which we will call the *plaintext*) and transforming it into a scrambled version of itself (which we will call the *ciphertext*). The theory goes that is it safe to have the ciphertext compromised, as an attacker will not be able to deduce the plaintext from only the scrambled form.

Symmetric Encryption

As a basic example, consider the Caesar Cipher, named after Julius Caesar, who is said to have invented it. If you want to transmit a message to your army, but are leary of your message being captured and read by your enemies en route, you could take each letter in the message and instead of writing that letter, write the letter that is x letters away from it. For example, let's supposed that Caesar and his generals decided to use an x value of 6. When Caesar wanted to send a message out, instead of writing an A, he would write the letter that is six (as $x=6$) letters away from A, which is G. Instead of writing a B, he would write an H. And so on. When the generals received this message, they would subtract six from each letter and recover the true message. Anyone intercepting the message would be unable to recover its true meaning, as they would not know what x is.

In this example, the true message is the plaintext. The shifted version of the message is the ciphertext. The algorithm used to encrypt the message is known as a shift cipher, as each character is shifted to another value, which is x away from the true value. The value of x is known as the *key*. Looking at this encryption system, one can go from the plaintext to the ciphertext (*encryption*) if one knows the algorithm used and the key. One can go back from the ciphertext to the plaintext (*decryption*) if one knows the algorithm and the key. The Caesar Cipher is a classic and very basic example of a *symmetric key encryption algorithm*, because the same key is used for both encryption and decryption.

The Caesar Cipher is very illustrative to how these symmetric key algorithms work. Even though this system is very old and easy to break nowadays, modern systems work along similar principles, where a plaintext message is sent in to an encryption algorithm along with a key, and the ciphertext comes out the other end. The most famous symmetric algorithm known today is probably the Data Encryption Standard (DES), which has been used for decades to protect information. It has largely been replaced by the Advanced Encryption Standard (AES), which is much newer and stronger. Today, AES is the standard for symmetric key encryption.

Symmetric encryption algorithms, AES and others, have similar principles. First, the algorithm itself is generally public and not a secret. The key, on the other hand, is very secret and must be protected. Anyone can recover the original message if they know the key used to encrypt a message. Second, the strength of the symmetric encryption is generally based on the length of the key used; the longer the key, the stronger the protection offered by the encryption. As of late 2011, the current standard key size is 256 bits (AES used with this size key is called AES-256). Third, symmetric encryption algorithms tend to be very fast; modern computers can encrypt and decrypt using them very quickly.

Let's look at the concept of symmetric encryption a bit more. These algorithms can be thought of as a box where you put in a message, locked by a key, and an encrypted message comes out when the key is used to unlock it. The process is reversible; the same key used to encrypt the message can decrypt the encrypted version. The longer the key you use, the harder it is to recover the original message from the encrypted one by brute force. Assuming you use a good size key and a good algorithm, you can store the encrypted message around your worse enemies all you want and they will be unable to recover the original message. Just protect that key!

Symmetric encryption is a great thing. However, there is one primary flaw with it. Think back to the Caesar Cipher. If Caesar wanted to use his algorithm to communicate securely with his generals, he would need to make sure that his generals out in the field had the same value of x that he did. (Otherwise, they would not be able to decrypt his messages.) Caesar cannot just send the key out via a message because his messages are being compromised, hence the whole need for this scheme. This is the primary flaw with symmetric encryption; it relies on all communicating parties having the same key before any messages are exchanged.

Asymmetric Key Encryption

Enter *asymmetric* key encryption. Symmetric key encryption carries that name because the same key is used for both encryption and decryption. Asymmetric key encryption uses two different keys: one for encryption and one for decryption. The keys have a special mathematical relationship that allows messages encrypted with one key to be decrypted by the other. As useful work with such keys revolves around their use with each other, we refer to them as *key pairs*.

In a typical asymmetric cryptography application, each communicating party has a key pair. It makes one key known to everyone in the world; this is known as the *public key*. It holds the other key, the *private key*, to itself and never divulges it. If someone wants to send a message to someone, they can protect the message by applying an asymmetrical encryption algorithm to it, using the recipient's public key. When the intended person receives the message, he can then use his private key to decrypt the message (remember, one key can decrypt messages encrypted using its partner key, so the private key can decrypt messages encrypted using its public key). The two parties did not need to exchange keys using some protected method before using encryption.

Asymmetric encryption algorithms are less plentiful than symmetric ones. The most common one is known as RSA, with each letter standing for the first letter of the last name of its three inventors. The algorithm itself is publicly known and not a secret. Each user's public key is also public knowledge and anyone can know it, but each user's private keys must be only accessible by that user. The strength of the asymmetric encryption, like symmetric encryption, is generally based on the length of the key used. However, the key lengths are not comparable between asymmetric and symmetric algorithms; RSA keys are generally considered (as of late 2011) to need to be at least 2048 bits long to offer protection comparable to that of AES-256. Also, asymmetric algorithms tend to be very slow, especially compared to symmetric ones, so the data being encrypted or decrypted should be minimized.

In summary, asymmetric encryption involves complementary encryption and decryption processes. Encryption requires the message and one member of the key pair. The process is reversible, but decryption requires the other member of the key pair. Assuming you use a good key size and a good algorithm, you can encrypt a message using someone's public key and only that person would be able to read it, no prior key sharing required.

Asymmetric key encryption has other uses, too. Instead of encrypting a message with someone else's public key (which allows only her to read it, as only she has the private key), what if you encrypted the message with your own private key? What benefit would that have? Well, say you write a message and want to prove that you are the author of it. You could release both the message and your encrypted form of it at the same time. Anyone can grab your public key (as it is public) and decrypt your encrypted form. If the published message comes out, you must be the author of the message. This scheme provides the basics for what is known as a digital signature, but that requires a bit more explanation first.

Cryptography Primer: Hashing

Encryption, be it symmetric or asymmetric, is a great thing. However, it is not the end-all-be-all of cryptography. Another important concept that you should be familiar with is a *hashing algorithm*. If you have studied data structures before, you are probably familiar with hash tables and similar organizational strategies. The key to using hash tables efficiently is the hashing function, which is applied to a piece of data and produces a result that is used to determine which of x hash buckets the data is to be stored. The general idea is that if there are x buckets, a good hash function will produce each result from 0 to x in equal frequency. A cryptographic hash is very similar, but this trait is taken further.

A *cryptographic hash function* takes a message of any length and produces a fixed-size hash called a digest. The digest looks like a random sequence of bits. For example, SHA-256 is a popular hashing function that produces 256-bit digests. You can put a message of any size, from a couple of bytes to multiple megabytes, into a SHA-256 function and the resulting digest value will always be 256 bits. The digest serves as a digital fingerprint of the message. Cryptographic hash computation is also very fast, roughly the same speed as symmetric cryptography.

All cryptographic hash functions have four main properties:

- If two digests are different, the two messages that produced them are different.
- If two digests are the same, it is highly likely that the two messages are the same.
- If a digest is computed on a message and a single bit of the message is changed, the digest produced will be completely different.
- It is computationally infeasible to find a message that will result in a specific digest.

Note that we said "highly likely" that two digests that are the same resulted from identical messages. Hash functions work on large inputs and produce small outputs. Therefore, there are a large number of messages that will produce the same digest (there have to be; there is an infinite number of possible inputs and only 2^x outputs, where x is the size of the digest). When two different messages produce the same digest, this is known as a *hash collision*. A good hash algorithm will minimize the number of collisions.

Notice also that hash functions are not reversible (as encryption functions are). They are known as *one-way functions*, as you can go one way (message to digest), but you cannot go back (digest to message).

So what could we use a cryptographic hash algorithm for? Let's look at two examples. One common use is to store credentials. When a user supplies a username and password, something must be able to determine whether the password is correct. One way this could be done would be to encrypt the users' passwords and decrypt the password of a specific user when they attempt to log in. Then, we can compare the password they supplied with the decrypted value and see if they match. However, this turns out to be a very bad idea. To encrypt and then decrypt user passwords, we would need to store and use a key (in this case, a symmetric key). If that key were to be compromised, all of the passwords for our users could be retrieved—a very bad outcome. Instead, passwords (or other credentials) should be hashed and the digest stored. When a user tries to authenticate, we hash the credential they supplied and compare it to the stored value; if they match, the user must have supplied the correct credential. Think back to our previous discussion about whether we need to store sensitive data: hashes make it possible to not store actual passwords.

Storing hashed passwords is somewhat more complex than simply hashing the password and storing that value. Modern implementations use functions that employ multiple rounds of hashing and the use of an additional protection mechanism known as a *salt*. We will discuss these two topics shortly.

Another common use of cryptographic hash algorithms is to verify data integrity. If you want to verify that a piece of data has not been altered, you can compute the hash of that data when it is stored and then do so again when it is accessed. If the hashes match, the data has not been altered. This application is why hashes are sometimes called a *cryptographic checksum*.

Finally, let's revisit the example we last discussed in the context of public key cryptography. We said that if a user wanted to prove he wrote a message, he could encrypt the message with his own private key and release that ciphertext along with the original message. Anyone could then use that user's public key to decrypt the ciphertext and if it matched the original message, we would know that the person did, in fact, write the message. However, think back to the properties of asymmetric encryption; it can be very slow to perform and the message in question may be quite long. To ameliorate this, apply hashing. Instead of encrypting the entire message with his private key, the author could hash the message and encrypt just the hash. Because digests are very small, the encryption should be very fast, as will the decryption necessary to verify the author's claims. This scheme—releasing an encrypted hash of a message to prove that you wrote it—is known as a *digital signature*.

Cryptographic Practicalities

Before we explore how to use cryptography to protect stored data in our Android applications, I need to explain a few more concepts.

Computational Infeasibility

We have used the term *computationally infeasible* a lot. This means that the amount of computing power needed to perform such a task is so great to make such an effort unlikely. As computing power increases, things that may have been infeasible decades ago become feasible. This is why cryptographic algorithms are always being updated, and key sizes tend to go up as time progresses. DES was the primary algorithm before AES and it stood strong for many years. However, DES was limited to a 56-bit key. As computers got faster, a brute-force attack against this small key size became possible. Here, computers would simply try every possible key (2^{56} of them) until they found the one that would properly decrypt the message. AES, on the other hand, can use different key sizes and 256-bit keys tend to be standard, as of late 2011. As computers keep advancing, this is likely to increase in the future.

Cryptographic hash algorithms have similar traits. MD5 was the hash function that saw widespread use before the SHA family of hashes came around, and it produces a 128-bit digest. The SHA family can produce hashes of different sizes and, again, a 256-bit digest is considered strong as of this writing, even though 512-bit hashes are fast becoming commonplace.

Algorithm Choice and Key Size

When choosing the algorithms and key sizes to use, one should use well-known, well-studied industry standard options. As I've said, for symmetric encryption, AES with 256-bit keys is the current standard. For asymmetric encryption, RSA with 2048-bit keys is the current standard. For hashing, SHA-256 is the current standard. (Its predecessor, SHA-1, is still in widespread use though it shouldn't be, and SHA-512 is becoming more and more common.) Once you decide which algorithms and key length to use, find and use a well-known and well-tested implementation. Do not, let's repeat this, *do not* write your own implementation of cryptographic algorithms. Getting them right is very tricky and small, subtle flaws can produce output that looks like it is working but offers protection that is nowhere near as strong as that offered by a proper implementation. (A good example of this is the CSS encryption scheme deployed on DVDs; flaws in that custom algorithm reduce its effectiveness considerably.)

It is important to keep in mind that different capabilities, including different cryptographic implementations, are added to Android all of the time. Different versions of Android will include different support for various cryptographic algorithms, and some versions may remove support for outdated algorithms as they become obsolete. This is another great reason why you need to test your application on multiple Android versions and multiple Android devices.

Do not write your own cryptography. The Android system provides a perfectly capable implementation of major cryptographic algorithms, which have been extensively tested and validated, so just use those.

Cipher Operation Modes, Initialization Vectors, and Salt

As we have discussed, encryption algorithms work on blocks of data (AES, for example, uses 128-bit blocks). One approach to encrypting a significant amount of data would be to just encrypt each block independently. There is a problem with this approach, however, as all blocks that contained identical data would encrypt to the same value and an attacker that could see the ciphertext would know that two blocks contained the same plaintext data. This would be bad, as it allows the attacker to learn something about the plaintext. To deal with this problem, encryption algorithms are typically performed in sequences, or modes, that make each block dependent on the previous block. For example, in *Cipher Block Chaining* (CBC) mode, each plaintext block is XORed with the previous ciphertext block and then encrypted. This ensures that plaintext blocks with the same contents encrypt to different ciphertext blocks. Note that we need something to XOR the very first block with to make this consistent. This value is known as an *initialization vector* (IV). It should be random, but it does not need to be secret, as the key does.

Along similar lines to IVs, applications of hashing algorithms typically involve the use of a *salt*. This is a value that is combined with the data being hashed (usually just concatenated with it) to make cracking a hash more difficult. Precomputed dictionary attacks against hashing algorithms consist of attackers using big tables (sometimes called rainbow tables) that list what common or likely passwords hash to, so they can look for a hash value they know and can determine if it was computed by hashing a common password very quickly. Including a random value (the salt) in the hash computation thwarts these types of attacks because the creation of such tables for data plus specific salt values would be computationally infeasible to compute and simply require too much space to store. Instead of computing a table where data1 hashes to hash1, you would need a table with data1+salt1 hashes to hash1, data1+salt2 hashes to hash2, and so on, for all possible hash values and salt values. Obviously, the longer the salt, the more effective it is; as of late 2011, sizes up to 128 bits of salt are common.

Just like with IVs, salt values should be random but they do not need to be kept secret. Indeed, this approach is used for password storage in countless systems: the salt value is stored along with the digest of the password for each user; the system looks up the salt, combines it with the submitted password, and hashes that to compare with the stored password digest. Note that the use of separate salt values for each password makes attacks even more difficult, as an attacker would need to brute-force crack each password hash individually if each one uses independent salt values.

Public Keys and Their Management

When it comes to asymmetric cryptography, we have said that users publish their public key so that anyone can see what it is. There is a problem here: how can I know what a user's public key really is? What if I publish my public key and then an attacker reads it and publishes it out as his own? There are two general strategies to remedy this problem.

The first is the *web of trust*, used by the popular encryption scheme known as Pretty Good Privacy (PGP). Here, I ask other users who already know me to digitally sign my public key along with my identity (usually an email address). The idea is that you may not know me, but you may know someone I know and if they signed my key, you trust their verification that it truly does belong to me. Or, maybe you don't know me or anyone that knows me, but you know someone who knows someone else who does know me. You can see where the "web" part of the web of trust comes from.

The other way of doing this is using *digital certificates*. We discussed this briefly earlier in the book, but let's revisit it here since we are talking about the management of public keys. Digital certificates involve the concept of the *trusted third party* (TTP). Using such a scheme, we all agree that some other party is going to vouch for everyone. That party verifies us and attests that our public keys really belong to us. If you would like to verify that the key I claim to be mine is, in fact, mine, you can ask the third party and they will show you what my public key is. This type of system is commonly implemented using digital certificates, which is just a standard way of including a public key, identity information, and the digital signature of the TTP in a standard package. Once I obtain a digital certificate, it has my identity and public key on it and it is digitally signed by a TTP that you trust. So you can rest assured that the public key is mine. This type of implementation is known as a *public key infrastructure* (PKI) and the entities that issue certificates are known as *certificate authorities* (CAs).

One common way of thinking about public keys, PKIs, and certificate authorities is to think of them as ID cards or, in the typical U.S. way of doing things these days, driver's licenses. Many people sign checks and legal documents everyday. To prove that the signature they have produced is, in fact, theirs, driver's licenses include a copy of the person's signature. They exist, among many other reasons, to serve as a document attesting to the fact that the person listed on the card has the signature that is also present on the card. In this case, the person listed on the card is the identity (the person) and the signature is the public key. (There is a whole separate argument about whether a driver's license is a good or appropriate way to do this, but that's not part of this discussion right now.) In the case of a PKI, a digital certificate is the license, the signature on the license is the public key, and the DMV (Department of Motor Vehicles) is the CA that issued the certificate. Grocery clerks, notaries, and others that are concerned with the validity of a person's signatures do not check to see if you, when you are signing a document, are really you in great detail. They have decided, along with most of society, to delegate that task to the DMV and the Trusted Third Party. Once the DMV verifies that you are you, they attest to that by issuing you a license. When you see a license, you have some trust that the DMV verified the person listed on it and the signature that appears on it belongs to the person listed. This is just like a digital certificate; the CA has verified that the person listed on it, and the public key included on it, match. This way you do not need to verify or trust that yourself. You just need to trust the Certificate Authority.

Key Derivation and Management

As you can see, cryptography offers us a vast set of tools that can be applied to solve data protection problems. One of the primary things that may be jumping out at you is the issue of keys and key management. Symmetric encryption can help mitigate a lot of risk involved with storing data on an Android device (indeed, we will look at some of these situations in just a little bit), but where does the key come from? Where do I store it? Or do I even need to store it? As you will soon see, key management is often the most difficult part of deploying cryptography on your app.

Motivation

Let's look at an old example, our social media aggregator app. Here we store sensitive data, the credentials of our user's social media accounts. We don't want someone unauthorized to be able to read that data, so we care about confidentiality. In this case, we can use encryption to mitigate the risk of compromise of the stored data. As we only have one entity (our app) ever accessing the data, a symmetric encryption algorithm is the appropriate choice. When our app stores a new or updated credential, it will first encrypt the username and password, then store the encrypted values. When the app needs to access those credentials to log in to the site in question, it will simply decrypt them at that point. The credentials will exist on the device only in encrypted form.

You may find yourself questioning the storing of a password, as we just said a few sections ago that we want to store the hash of a password and never the actual value. In that case, however, we only ever wanted to verify that the password a user gave us later was the correct value (someone was authenticating to us). In that case, we do not need to store the password because we can compare the digests to know if the supplied password is valid. In this case, however, we are going to send the actual password to a third party (the social media network). They do not accept hash digests, but only real passwords (and rightly so), so we need to store the actual password so we can decrypt it and send it to the social network server.

Key Derivation

This is remarkably easy to code up (we will see an example of that in just a bit). However, in order to do so, we need to supply a key to the encryption API calls. If we generated a random key and stored it along with the encrypted data, this would nullify the protection offered by encrypting the data (and would be very much like buying a strong deadbolt lock for your front door and leaving the key taped to the door). So this is not a good solution.

Reverse Engineering

Storing an encryption key along with the encrypted data renders the protection offered by the encryption almost moot. This is never a good idea and only slightly increases the work an attacker would need to put in to recover the data. The reason for this is that Android applications can be *reverse engineered*. Applications are packaged into an APK file, which contains compiled code and resources. There are multiple tools available (and multiple tutorials on the Web giving a step-by-step procedure on how to do all of this) that can take an APK file and recover all of the contents, easily showing anyone that is interested how an application works, the hardcoded values that are present (including any encryption keys), database connection strings, and so on. It is never a good idea to rely on *security by obscurity*, where you assume that an attacker cannot figure out how your application works as a defense mechanism...an attacker can always figure out how your application works and any of the values contained within. As a consequence, your risk analysis should assume that an attacker has full

---

knowledge of all of this information and your application should be designed to resist assault from attackers with this knowledge (hence, why it is very important to not store keys in your application).

It is possible to provide some protection for the contents of your APK, and the design that could be revealed by reverse engineering it, by *obfuscating* it. This refers to an automated procedure (there are multiple tools available that can do it) that takes your application and turns it into a functionally equivalent version that is very difficult to understand. This makes it so that an attacker who is attempting to reverse engineer your application could recover the code, but it would be very confusing and more difficult for them to understand, hiding the original design. However, it will still run the same as your original well-designed version, so this is not a panacea against this threat.

Also, keep in mind that reverse engineering is not specific to Android. *Anything* can be reverse engineered, given enough time and effort. While this process is easier in environments like Android and Java, and it is more difficult in environments such as compiled C or C++ code, this is a threat against all applications. You can never prevent reverse engineering, but you can make it much more difficult and much more costly (especially in terms of time required), using techniques such as obfuscation.

The solution to this problem is to derive the key when it is needed. Your app will need to prompt the user for a credential (usually a password) and then use that value to form the key. Basically, you need to take a variable-length input (the credential) and come up with a fixed-length output (the key). Furthermore, it should be very unlikely that two different passwords would produce the same key. Sound like anything to you? Yes, this is the very definition of a hash algorithm. Older methods of key derivation typically did this (and only this), and modern techniques are based on similar principles.

In this case, we need to use a *key derivation function* (KDF) designed for password-based encryption (PBE). There are a number of standard ways to do this, composed of multiple iterations of hashing, performed on the password combined with salt. The resulting value is then used as a key for subsequent encryption computations. All of this complexity, the inclusion of salt plus a large number of iterations, serves to make cracking the password (using a technique that looks at the key and attempts to compute the password that will result in it) much more difficult than it would be if a single hash computation was used.

Android includes a good PBE algorithm that uses SHA-256 and AES, standardized and strong algorithms, to compute a symmetric key from a password through hashing, encryption computations, and multiple rounds. To form a key from a String (such as a password), add something like this to your code:

```
String password = ...;

String PBE_ALGORITHM = "PBEWithSHA256And256BitAES-CBC-BC";
int NUM_OF_ITERATIONS = 1000;
int KEY_SIZE = 256;
```

```
byte[] salt = "abababababababababababab".getBytes();

try
{
    PBEKeySpec pbeKeySpec = new PBEKeySpec(password.toCharArray(),
        salt, NUM_OF_ITERATIONS, KEY_SIZE);
    SecretKeyFactory keyFactory = SecretKeyFactory.getInstance(PBE_ALGORITHM);
    SecretKey tempKey = keyFactory.generateSecret(pbeKeySpec);
    SecretKey secretKey = new SecretKeySpec(tempKey.getEncoded(), "AES");
}
catch (Exception exp)
{
    ...
}
```

In order to fully understand how the key derivation works, let's go through this code and point out the relevant portions.

```
String PBE_ALGORITHM = "PBEWithSHA256And256BitAES-CBC-BC";
int NUM_OF_ITERATIONS = 1000;
int KEY_SIZE = 256;
```

This section of the code just sets up what algorithms and parameters we are going to use. In this case, we will use the built-in Password Based Encryption key derivation function (PBE), using SHA-256 as the hashing algorithm and AES as the encryption algorithm. The CBC denotation in the algorithm specification indicates that we are using AES in Cipher Block Chaining mode, which is a standard way of using AES when dealing with data that is composed of multiple 128-bit blocks. We will use 1,000 iterations of the hashing function during the process (NUM_OF_ITERATIONS), as this is generally considered to be a secure number and will make current brute-force attacks computationally infeasible, and will end up with a 256-bit key (KEY_SIZE). These are standard parameters and will result in a strong key.

```
byte[] salt = "abababababababababababab".getBytes();
```

Here, we set up the salt that will be used in the key derivation computation. As you'll recall, the salt is concatenated with the value being hashed to make cracking the password harder to accomplish. In this case, the value of the salt can be anything and does not need to be kept secret, so we will just hardcode a particular value. In order to always derive the same key from the same password, we need to make sure that the salt is the same every time; this is why we hardcode it into our program. Note that we are only doing this for an example; a more ideal implementation would compute and store this salt value during the first run of the application on a particular device. This would enable each device to have a salt value that is unique to that device, which is a stronger implementation.

```
PBEKeySpec pbeKeySpec = new PBEKeySpec(password.toCharArray(),
    salt, NUM_OF_ITERATIONS, KEY_SIZE);
SecretKeyFactory keyFactory = SecretKeyFactory.getInstance(PBE_ALGORITHM);
SecretKey tempKey = keyFactory.generateSecret(pbeKeySpec);
SecretKey secretKey = new SecretKeySpec(tempKey.getEncoded(), "AES");
```

Here we actually generate the key. First, we create a PBEKeySpec object that contains all of the parameters we just set up, including the password we are going to derive the key from, the salt value, the number of iterations we want to use in our computation, and the size of the key we want to derive. We then create a SecretKeyFactory that specifies the algorithm we will use (AES in Cipher Block Chaining mode). The PBE-KeySpec is then passed in to the SecretKeyFactory to generate a secret value, which is then encoded for use with AES (because we will be using AES to perform our actual encryption, which we will implement in a later section). The resulting 256-bit key, encoded for use with AES encryption, is referred to using the secretKey variable.

And that's it. We have now generated a symmetric key from a password. This is the same process your app will go through whenever the user wants to access sensitive data; they will input their password and you will derive the symmetric key in this manner. The actual encryption and decryption of the data will be discussed in the next section, in a complete example.

Encryption Without User-Supplied Key Derivation

We have now seen how to derive an encryption key based on some user-supplied data. When we need to encrypt or decrypt stored data, we would need to prompt the user for her password and run it though a KDF, as we have just seen. Practically, it would make for a very bad user experience if we prompted the user for her password every time we needed to store or read a single piece of data. So what is frequently done is to prompt the user when our application starts up, derive the key, and then cache it. While this does alter our risk calculation and reduce the security of our solution, it is a tradeoff that makes sense for a vast majority of scenarios. Of course, there may very well be a situation where the data being stored is of ultra-high sensitivity and we may want to prompt the user for her password before every write or read of it; again, it is all a matter of applying appropriate safeguards for a given level of risk.

So what if you do not want to prompt the user for a password at all, but your app needs to perform encryption or decryption operations? Unfortunately, there is no straightforward solution here for an Android app. You need keys to perform encryption, so you need to have either the key or something you can derive the key from (the password, in our examples). If you do not want the user to supply that critical piece of information, you need to store it within the app (or somewhere else on the device). This practice (storing a hardcoded key within the app) is not a secure way of handling things, because an attacker can easily look through your app's code to learn the key and thus compromise the data. (Android apps provide little to no protection against reverse engineering, where an attacker can take a compiled application and recover the source code for it.) Unfortunately, Android just does not offer a better solution at this time; there is no super safe place you can store that key or password so that someone with access to the device cannot get it.

Keep in mind that protections must be appropriate for the given level of risk. For sensitive data like passwords, storing the encryption keys hardcoded into the application is a poor choice and should not be done as that data is highly sensitive. If, however, the goal is simply to make things a little more difficult for a casual attacker, as opposed to someone with high levels of motivation to recover the data your application is storing, such an approach may be appropriate. There is a big difference between storing data unencrypted on a removable media card and storing it encrypted with the key embedded in the application that is installed on the device itself. In this case, we are deploying a countermeasure to the loss of the media card, as opposed to an attacker that would have access to both the phone (where the key exists) and the media card (where the data exists). Is this protection effective against a determined attacker? No. Do not confuse yourself into thinking that storing a hardcoded encryption key within your application is *ever* secure; it amounts to obfuscation and little more. But again, apply appropriate safeguards for the level of risk you are trying to address, and that is all based on the data your application is storing.

Another option to consider is off-device storage. The problems we are discussing in this chapter exist because there are no good ways, native to Android, to store sensitive data on the device. We can solve this problem using tools like encryption, but we then need to either prompt the user to supply credentials to generate the key whenever we need it (resulting in a slightly degraded user experience) or store the keys on the device (resulting in an incomplete and insecure storage solution). If your app can instead make a trusted and protected connection back to a server and then ask that server for its key every time it needs to perform an encryption or decryption operation, the key storage problem goes away. This approach, however, opens up a whole new set of challenges that we will discuss in the next chapter.

Practical Cryptography: Applying a Technique Against a Threat

Now that we understand the basics behind the primary cryptographic tools we have at our disposal, let's look at a full data protection situation. Here we need to store sensitive data, and we need to protect it from compromise. We care about the confidentiality and integrity of this data. It should be safe even if it is stored on an external storage media card (which, as we discussed before, does not enjoy the isolation offered by the Linux base) or a rooted phone (where other apps may run with permissions that allow them to bypass such controls). We need to encrypt the data. When the app needs to access the data, we will prompt the user for a password, derive the symmetric encryption key from that password, and then decrypt the data (to read it) or encrypt it (to store it).

We have already seen much of the code to do this when we discussed key derivation functions. Here is the complete listing that will allow the encryption or decryption of data based on a password:

```
String password = ...;

String PBE_ALGORITHM = "PBEWithSHA256And256BitAES-CBC-BC";
String CIPHER_ALGORITHM = "AES/CBC/PKCS5Padding";
int NUM_OF_ITERATIONS = 1000;
int KEY_SIZE = 256;

byte[] salt = "ababababababababababab".getBytes();
byte[] iv = "1234567890abcdef".getBytes();

String clearText = ...; // This is the value to be encrypted.
byte[] encryptedText;
byte[] decryptedText;

try
{
    PBEKeySpec pbeKeySpec = new PBEKeySpec(password.toCharArray(),
        salt, NUM_OF_ITERATIONS, KEY_SIZE);
    SecretKeyFactory keyFactory = SecretKeyFactory.getInstance(PBE_ALGORITHM);
    SecretKey tempKey = keyFactory.generateSecret(pbeKeySpec);
    SecretKey secretKey = new SecretKeySpec(tempKey.getEncoded(), "AES");

    IvParameterSpec ivSpec = new IvParameterSpec(iv);

    Cipher encCipher = Cipher.getInstance(CIPHER_ALGORITHM);
    encCipher.init(Cipher.ENCRYPT_MODE, secretKey, ivSpec);

    Cipher decCipher = Cipher.getInstance(CIPHER_ALGORITHM);
    decCipher.init(Cipher.DECRYPT_MODE, secretKey, ivSpec);

    encryptedText = encCipher.doFinal(clearText.getBytes());

    decryptedText = decCipher.doFinal(encryptedText);
    String sameAsClearText = new String(decryptedText);
}
catch (Exception e)
{
    ...
}
```

In order to fully understand how the various components of encrypting and decrypting data work, let's go through this code and point out the relevant portions:

```
String PBE_ALGORITHM = "PBEWithSHA256And256BitAES-CBC-BC";
String CIPHER_ALGORITHM = "AES/CBC/PKCS5Padding";
int NUM_OF_ITERATIONS = 1000;
int KEY_SIZE = 256;
```

This section of the code just sets up the algorithms and parameters we are going to use. In this case, we use the same key derivation parameters we previously discussed, with SHA-256 as the hashing algorithm and AES in CBC mode as the encryption algorithm. We will use 1,000 iterations of the hashing function during the process (NUM_OF_ITERA TIONS) and will end up with a 256-bit key (KEY_SIZE). We also now specify the algorithm to use for the actual encryption and decryption of data. We will be using AES, still in

Cipher Block Chaining mode, and employ PKCS#5 padding (a standardized method of padding a message to be encrypted). The padding setting specified how to pad the data being encrypted (or decrypted) if it is not in multiples of 128 bits, as AES operates on blocks of 128 bits at a time. These are all standard algorithms and parameters, representing a strong encryption scheme (as of late 2011, anyway).

```
byte[] salt = "abababababababababababab".getBytes();
byte[] iv = "1234567890abcdef".getBytes();
```

Here, we set up the salt that will be used in the key derivation computation and the Initialization Vector (IV) that will be used in encryption and decryption of data. We have already discussed the role of salt in computations involving hashing and the role of IVs in starting encryption when using a mode (like CBC) that chains blocks together. Just as with a salt, it can be anything and does not need to be kept secret, so we will just hardcode a particular value. In order to always derive the same key from the same password, we need to make sure that the IV, just like the salt, is the same every time; this is why we hardcode it into our code.

Note that in this implementation, we are using a static IV to encrypt the data we are storing. Remember what an IV is used for: it is designed so that if you encrypt the same plaintext using the same key, you'll end up with a different ciphertext if you use a different IV. If you use the same IV, and encrypt the same plaintext with the same key, you'll end up with the same ciphertext. For stored data, this is not a huge deal, but if you're using this to build a communications protocol, you will want to use different and random IVs each time you send a message. That way someone observing your encrypted communications cannot tell if you send the same message more than once (remember, we don't want to give away any information about the contents of our encrypted messages, that is why we are encrypting them).

```
String clearText = ...; // This is the value to be encrypted.
byte[] encryptedText;
byte[] decryptedText;
```

Here, we just set up the values we will encrypt and decrypt. For the purpose of this example, clearText will hold the String we want to encrypt before we store. encrypted Text is a byte array that will hold the encrypted value of the String. Finally, decrypted Text will hold the decrypted bytes, once we encrypt the string and then decrypt it.

```
PBEKeySpec pbeKeySpec = new PBEKeySpec(password.toCharArray(),
    salt, NUM_OF_ITERATIONS, KEY_SIZE);
SecretKeyFactory keyFactory = SecretKeyFactory.getInstance(PBE_ALGORITHM);
SecretKey tempKey = keyFactory.generateSecret(pbeKeySpec);
SecretKey secretKey = new SecretKeySpec(tempKey.getEncoded(), "AES");
```

Here, we perform key derivation, going from the user-supplied password to a 256-bit AES key, just as we discussed in the last section.

```
IvParameterSpec ivSpec = new IvParameterSpec(iv);
```

We then set up the Initialization Vector (IV).

```
Cipher encCipher = Cipher.getInstance(CIPHER_ALGORITHM);
encCipher.init(Cipher.ENCRYPT_MODE, secretKey, ivSpec);

Cipher decCipher = Cipher.getInstance(CIPHER_ALGORITHM);
decCipher.init(Cipher.DECRYPT_MODE, secretKey, ivSpec);
```

This is the guts of our example. We use the derived key and the IV, along with our specification of what encryption parameters we want to use, to form a Cipher object. We actually create two, one in ENCRYPT_MODE and one in DECRYPT_MODE. With the exception of that mode, the Cipher objects are created in exactly the same manner.

```
encryptedText = encCipher.doFinal(clearText.getBytes());
```

Once we have the Cipher objects, we can perform encryption and decryption operations. First, we will encrypt. We pass the String we want to encrypt (converted into a byte array) to the doFinal() method of the encrypting Cipher object. The encryption operation is performed and the resulting encrypted bytes are returned to us. That's all there is to it.

```
decryptedText = decCipher.doFinal(encryptedText);
String sameAsClearText = new String(decryptedText);
```

We can also decrypt data using the same approach. In this case, we use the decrypting Cipher object, passing it the encrypted bytes and getting back to plaintext bytes. As we started with a String, we can reconstruct it, and the sameAsClearText String will contain exactly the same value as the clearText string.

And that's it. We now have a complete solution for protecting stored data, where we take a user-supplied password, derive a symmetric key from it, and encrypt and decrypt data at will, all in a few short lines of code. Once we encrypt the data, we can store it in a file, in a database, or wherever. As long as we keep the symmetric key from compromise (as in, do not store it anywhere at any time), an attacker will not be able to recover the data from its encrypted form.

CHAPTER 6

Securing Server Interactions

The previous chapters have all dealt with data stored on the Android device. Now, we move on to securing data transmission off of the device to other parties, notably servers that the client application interacts with. In this case, we make use of some of the cryptographic constructs that we introduced previously, and look at mechanisms that Android shares with other common platforms. As always, the risk analysis of the data we are transferring over the network will dictate the level of protection we need to include.

Confidentiality and Authentication

When data is being sent off of the device to somewhere else, a security-minded developer must consider two primary considerations. The first is *authentication*. In this context, we refer to the capability of verifying that the entity we are communicating with, either sending data to or receiving data from, is the entity that we think it is. This is important for many reasons. First, we may want ensure that a computer to which we are uploading data from the device is an entity that should have it. Thus, in our example of a social media aggregator, we should send the Facebook username and password only to a Facebook server. Otherwise, we may be exposing confidential data to a party that should not have access to it, which must be avoided. Also, we may want to download data only from a trusted source. If our social media aggregator does not verify that the server it is talking to really belongs to Facebook, we may display an update to the user that comes from a rogue source—which in turn may cause the user to take action he should not take. These examples illustrate the point, but they are not worst-case scenarios; our apps must be able to verify that the entities they are communicating with are, in fact, the entities they claim to be.

The other consideration is the *confidentiality* of the data being transmitted over the network. This refers to steps that prevent a third-party from reading the data while it is being transmitted. In the case of our social media aggregator app, we do not want someone uninvolved in the transaction to be able to view the user's social media credentials as they are sent from the device to the Facebook server. Going in the other direction, we do not want financial data sent from a bank server to our app running on an Android device to be read by another party who happens to have access to a critical part of the cellular data network.

SSL/TLS: The Industry Standard

The gold standard in protecting data in transit over the Internet is the *Secure Sockets Layer (SSL)* and its successor, *Transport Layer Security (TLS)*. This protocol is designed to provide the two critical services I laid out in the preceding section: protecting the confidentiality of data as it is transported across a network and allowing the client to authenticate the server it is communicating with, so that it knows it is sending data to, and receiving data from, the correct entity. It is also possible to use SSL/TLS to allow the server to authenticate the client, in a reversal of the traditional mechanism.

Note that this section, and most of this chapter, talks about protecting data that is sent between the client (your Android application) and a server. Included in this discussion is device authentication—letting the server verify it is actually talking to the client it thinks it is and also allowing the client to verify that it is actually talking to the server it thinks it is. Authentication *of a user* is not part of this discussion, but is something that you should consider when designing your application and the system it will be a part of.

Many applications require a user to provide a username and password to authenticate the user. While commonplace, this requires the credentials to be passed to the server every time, which even when done so over an encrypted channel, is not ideal. Better solutions do exist, and are supported within Android, that allow the client to generate a token and send that to a server for ongoing authentication. The AccountManager class in Android allows your application to use a token to authenticate to the servers in question. Indeed, this is how the Google applications authenticate the user to Google's servers rather than pass the username and password over the channel all of the time. This is a much stronger approach to credential management and usage. Designing your application to use AccountManager and an Authenticator is a strong approach for user authentication and should be used instead of passing usernames and passwords, if possible.

Authentication of the Entities

The first primary function of SSL/TLS is to enable the client to verify that it is, in fact, conversing with the entity (the server) that it thinks it is. When a client browses to a hostname (or an IP address), it has a reasonable expectation that the entity it is conversing with is the one that belongs to that hostname (again, or IP address). However, there are a whole slew of attacks and techniques that can be used to force that communication to occur with other rogue entities. (The nature and types of these compromises are not vital to an understanding of this topic, so we will not discuss them here, but realize that just because your app attempts to connect to a server with a specific hostname or IP address, the entity that responds back may not be the one you think it is.) SSL/TLS uses asymmetric key cryptography and (optionally) a public key infrastructure to provide this server authentication service, as we will discuss later.

One of the first steps in an SSL/TLS communication involves the server sending its digital certification to the client. This certificate is used to identify the client and typically includes the server name, the name of the certificate authority that issued the certificate, and the public key that belongs to the server. At this point, a client can decide to verify that the certificate presented is correct and valid, or can choose to decline to perform this validation. Clients should always perform the validation to make sure that the certificate really was signed by the CA that the server claims issued it and that the certificate is not a forgery. There are, however, plenty of client implementations that do not perform this step.

Once the client verifies that the server's certificate is valid, it will generate a random number, using whatever random number generation routines are present on the client's platform. It will encrypt that random number using the public key provided by the server as part of its digital certificate and then send the encrypted value back to the server. The server will then use its private key, which only it has access to, to decrypt that random number. This step verifies that the client is, in fact, communicating with the server that it thinks it is, the one identified in the digital certificate.

Because a certificate authority has issued this certificate specifying the public key used and the server identity, and we trust the CA, we know that the public key in question does, in fact, belong to the server listed. If we encrypt a value with that public key, only the entity that has access to the corresponding private key will be able to decrypt it. So if we verify that the certificate that the server presents is, in fact, valid and we encrypt something with the contained public key, only the entity listed on the certificate will be able to decrypt our value, and the same random number will be present on both the server and the client (if the server was not in possession of the corresponding private key, it would not be able to decrypt the value successfully and would, therefore, not be able to know the value in question). This random number is used to generate a shared secret key between the client and the server, so only they can compute the shared secret key (the *master secret*). After this handshake occurs, the client and the server communicate using symmetric encryption that uses the key derived from the master secret, and the client knows that it must be communicating with the server it thinks it is.

Also possible with SSL/TLS, but not nearly as common, is for the server to authenticate the client in addition to the client authenticating the server. SSL/TLS was originally designed with ecommerce in mind, where many clients (users running web browsers) would connect to a few number of servers (the ecommerce storefronts). In this case, the server does not care who is talking to it, but the client absolutely cares which server it is talking to. However, SSL/TLS does provide for a server to authenticate the client, in cases where the server may want to communicate only with a select group. In this case, a digital certificate that belongs to the client is sent as part of the SSL/TLS handshake. This certificate contains the same kind of information as the server's certificate, but identifying the client, and the communications from the server to the client make use of the public key contained within the certificate. So only clients who possess the private key that corresponds to the public key contained in the certificate can successfully decrypt the data from the server (this is a one-to-one parallel with how server authentication is done). Client-authenticated SSL/TLS is rarely done, because most clients do not have digital certificates with which to identify themselves (indeed, server owners pay a significant amount of money to the CA that issues their identity digital certificate to compensate them for the verification that they perform). However, if a server does want to authenticate the clients that attempt to communicate with it, this is a technique that can be used. The need to supply clients with a digital certificate to use for identity purposes, either from a commercial certificate authority or from a private certificate server that you can stand up yourself, is somewhat problematic, as we will see in a later section.

Encryption of Data

Once an SSL/TLS handshake is complete, and the master secret has been computed by both the client and the server, symmetric encryption keys are derived from this value. The exact method by which this happens is not relevant to programmers who use SSL/TLS, as opposed to those that design and study it, so we need not discuss it here. Once the symmetric encryption keys are derived, each message between the client and the server is encrypted using them, typically by applying a stream-based encryption algorithm. SSL/TLS messages also typically include a Message Authentication Code (MAC) that is a construct of the message itself and a secret value derived from the master secret; this allows the recipient of the message to verify its authenticity. Note that successful decryption of the message by the recipient already implies this; the inclusion of the MAC is optional and derived from an option to use SSL/TLS while specifying a null cipher, where encryption would not be performed.

Using null ciphers with SSL/TLS removes the protection offered by the encryption. Such a configuration should never be used in practice. (It may be used during testing of a new application, but even better approaches to testing and debugging exist.)

Protecting Data En Route to Public Services

Now that we know how the SSL/TLS protocols work, we can look at the implementation in Android and how we will set up a secure connection between our application and the server it is talking to. For the purposes of this discussion, we are going to assume we are talking to a public server, meaning one that is using an SSL/TLS server certificate issued by a commercial Certificate Authority, whose root is trusted by the Android system by default. When Google releases Android builds, they include the root CA certificates from many different providers, all of which issue commercial certificates to entities that prove their identity for their servers. If we need to open up a secure communications path (encrypted to protect the confidentiality of the data and authenticated to make sure we are communicating with the server we think we are), the code required is minimal.

Introducing the Android SSL/TLS Environment

The standard way to set up an SSL/TLS-protected communications channel to a server is to use the HttpsURLConnection class. This is a class derived from the standard HttpURL Connection class, but implements SSL/TLS for the connection using the standard Android SSL/TLS configuration. The easiest way to open a connection using HTTP over SSL/TLS is to call openConnection() on a URL object, specifying the HTTPS protocol:

```
URL url = new URL("https://clientaccess.example.com");
HttpsURLConnection urlConn = (HttpsURLConnection)url.openConnection();
```

Or alternatively, you can create a HttpsURLConnection directly:

```
HttpsURLConnection urlConn = new HttpsURLConnection("https://
clientaccess.example.com");
```

After the HttpsURLConnection is open, you can use it just like a regular HttpURLConnection:

```
try
{
    URL url = new URL("https://clientaccess.example.com");
    HttpsURLConnection urlConn = (HttpsURLConnection)url.openConnection();
    urlConn.setDoOutput(true);
    OutputStream output = urlConn.getOutputStream();
    InputStream input = urlConn.getInputStream();
}
```

And that's it. As you can see, opening a SSL/TLS-protected connection to a server using a trusted CA-issued certificate is just as easy as opening up a regular HTTP connection. Once you do have an SSL/TLS connection, you can examine various data about it, because the HttpsURLConnection class exposes much of that information. Rarely would you actually need to know it, but it can be helpful for testing, and it is good to know that you can get access to it should you want to. Here are a couple examples of information that you can get from the HttpsURLConnection object:

getCipherSuite()
> This method returns the cipher suite (which cryptographic algorithms are in use) for this connection. This tells you the strength of the underlying protection mechanism for this communications path.

getServerCertificates()
> This method returns an array of all of the certificates that the server supplied as identifying information. This allows you to view the entire chain of certificates from

the root CA (which your application trusts because Android trusts it) to the certificate for the actual server you are communicating with.

Server Verification

One of the features of SSL/TLS is *hostname verification*. When an SSL/TLS connection is set up, the SSL/TLS environment compares the hostname of the server you are attempting to connect to (*clientaccess.example.com* in our above example) to the certificate that is presented by the server itself. If the verification passes (using whatever hostname verification rules are enabled; more about this later), you can be assured that the connection was established just fine. However, if the hostname specified in the URL does not match the hostname in the certificate presented by the server, the connection will fail with an exception. This is intended to make sure that you are connecting to the server that you think you are. So connections to *clientaccess.example.com* require the server to which you are connecting to actually supply a *clientaccess.example.com* certificate and not one with a different name.

The hostname verification function is implemented by classes that make use of the `HostnameVerifier` interface. Android includes a few concrete classes that implement this interface and perform hostname verification in different ways:

AllowAllHostnameVerifier
> This hostname verifier basically turns hostname verification off. As long as the certificate that is presented by the server is trusted (i.e. comes from a trusted CA), it will be accepted regardless of whether the hostname in the URL matches the name on the certificate. As I said earlier, many clients skip verification in this manner, but I recommend that you take the extra time and traffic to do the verification.

StrictHostnameVerifier
> This hostname verifier is the same as the verification in the default (non-Android) Java releases. It checks the first CN present in the server certificate against the hostname specified in the URL and also checks all of the subject-alt entries in the certificate for a match. Wildcards are allowed, but only up to one level. For example, `*.example.com` would match *server1.example.com*, but not *server1.domain1.example.com*).

BrowserCompatHostnameVerifier
> This hostname verifier is just like `StrictHostnameVerifier`, but wildcards in the certificate name will match multiple levels. For example, `*.example.com` would match *server1.domain1.example.com* in this method, whereas `StrictHostnameVerifier` would reject it.

If you want to implement hostname verification for certificates using some type of verification not present in one of these providers, simply create your own `HostnameVerifier` class. All you need to do is implement the `HostnameVerifier` interface. It has only one method—`verify()`—which takes in the URL to verify an `SSLSession` object, from which you can obtain the name on the certificate. Perform whatever verification logic you want to and return a Boolean value to indicate whether the certificate should be accepted or not. A complete implementation may look like this:

```
HostnameVerifier customHV = new HostnameVerifier()
{
    public boolean verify(String urlHostname, SSLSession connSession)
    {
        String certificateHostname = connSession.getPeerHost();

        // compare urlHostname and certificateHostname here and
        // return true if the certificate should be accepted and
        // false if it should be rejected.
    }
};
```

Once you have a `HostnameVerifier` object, either by using one of the provided implementations or by creating your own, you need to configure the SSL/TLS environment to use it when making new SSL/TLS connections. To do this, simply call `setDefaultH ostnameVerifier()`, a static method of the `HttpsURLConnection` class. Any future SSL/ TLS connections will make use of the specified `HostnameVerifier`:

```
HostnameVerifier newHV = new StrictHostnameVerifier();
HttpsURLConnection.setDefaultHostnameVerifier(newHV);
```

Using HostnameVerifier for Other Purposes

It is important to keep in mind that hostname verification and certificate trust are two different things. In order for an SSL/TLS connection to be established, both checks must pass. First, the certificate that the server presents must be trusted; in most cases that means it must have been issued by a trusted Certificate Authority. Second, the hostname verification must match; this means that the name on the certificate must match the hostname you are trying to connect to. These are separate issues.

That being said, it is entirely possible to use any criteria you want to make a decision within a custom `HostnameVerifier`. For example, suppose you wanted to reject certificates issued by a particular CA that is, by default, trusted in Android. You could create a `TrustManager` that would trust every CA that is normally trusted by default except for the one in question (we'll see this approach shortly). But that is a lot of manual effort. You could instead choose to look at the CA that has issued the certificate within the HostnameVerifier and choose to reject the verification if the certificate in question was issued by the CA you do not want to trust. Here is an example:

```
HostnameVerifier customHV = new HostnameVerifier()
    {
        public boolean verify(String urlHostname, SSLSession connSession)
        {
            boolean isCertOK = true;

            String certificateHostname = connSession.getPeerHost();
            // If we want to, can check to see the name of the host we connected to
            // and make a decision based on that information on if we trust it.
```

```
                try {
                    Certificate[] certs = connSession.getPeerCertificates();
                    X509Certificate caCert = (X509Certificate)(certs[certs.length - 1]);
                    String caName = caCert.getIssuerX500Principal().getName();

                    if ( caName == CA_WE_DO_NOT_WANT_TO_TRUST )
                    // Check to see if the certificate was issued by a CA that we
                    // choose to reject. If so, we'll reject it.
                    {
                        isCertOK = false;
                    }
                }
                catch (SSLPeerUnverifiedException e)
                // If we cannot verify the host, reject it.
                {
                    isCertOK = false;
                }

                return isCertOK;
            }
        };
```

As you can see, you can do pretty much any check you want within a HostnameVerifier to make the decision to accept or reject. The criteria you choose, and how you choose to enforce them, is entirely up to you based on the risk analysis for your application.

Handling SSL/TLS Connection Errors

As we have discussed, when attempting to make SSL/TLS connections, two primary errors can come up. First, checking the trust in a server certificate may fail if the certificate is not issued by a trusted CA. Second, verifying the hostname may fail if the hostname in the connection URL is not the same as that specified on the server's certificate.

In the case of server certificate trust, an attempt to connect will result in an SSLExcep tion with the exception text indicating that a "not trusted server certificate" was provided. So if this happens, what should the client application do? The answer is very simple: don't communicate with that server. At this point, some developers think that the solution is to use a standard HTTP connection instead of the protected HTTPS one. This would completely remove the protections for confidentiality and authentication that SSL/TLS provides. Indeed, think about what such a decision would mean: you are unable to verify that the server you are talking to is the one you think it is, so you just ignore that and talk to them anyway? This is not a very secure or safe practice!

Indeed, it's possible that nothing at all could be wrong. Perhaps the server in question is using an expired certificate (which can cause the same error), or there has been a misconfiguration by those maintaining the server. These cases are entirely possible, but we cannot know for sure. All we know is that we could not verify the server's identity. So, we should not communicate with it. Period.

It can be difficult to keep server certificates up-to-date and configured correctly. Whenever a certificate expires, browsers will display an error when they connect to it. If a certificate does not exactly match the name entered into a browser (e.g. a request to *example.com* resulting in a certificate for *www.example.com* coming back), browsers will display an error. These two situations are the cause of a lot of false alerts that people see from their browsers (innocent mistakes causing user warnings).

The same can be said of hostname verification. This check makes sure that the certificate being presented matches the one for which you asked. Suppose you walked into a conference room and asked for Mr. Smith. A man claiming to be him gets up and shows you his identification, which reads Mr. Taylor. Do you trust that man is the one you are looking for, just because he responded to your query for Mr. Smith and had a valid driver's license? Of course you don't. And your client application should do the same. Hostname verification, like server certificate trust checking, is done for a reason and is critical to the authentication function of SSL/TLS. If your application receives a failure in either one of these checks, do not communicate further with that server, plain and simple.

Making sure that certificates presented by a server are trusted (issued by a trusted CA in the case of public-facing servers) and performing hostname verification are critical to the authentication function of SSL/TLS. If you cannot verify who you are talking to, stop talking to them!

Protecting Data En Route to Private Services

The previous section showed how to protect data en route to public services, where our application may need to connect to a wide range of servers and/or these servers may be out of our control. In those cases, validation of the SSL/TLS certificates used by those servers is accomplished using the built-in Android PKI support and relies on these servers using certificates that are signed in a chain that begins with a root CA certificate included with Android. This model works well when we need to communicate with servers that do so, but has a lot of issues when we are communicating with only one specific server (or a small group of them), all of which are under our control and are built to serve the client application. We will now look at how we can modify the configuration of the Android SSL/TLS implementation to restrict which server certificates will be trusted, to enable the trust of self-signed certificates, and to use client certificates to identify our client application to the server.

Using Only Specific Certificates for SSL/TLS

The standard SSL/TLS environment accepts all server certificates that are issued by a trusted Certificate Authority, and the Android system contains a long list of certificates for CAs to trust. When data is being exchanged with specific servers, the SSL/TLS environment can be configured to allow only specific certificates to be used. This allows you to lock down the servers that your application can connect. It also lets you configure the SSL/TLS environment to trust certificates that are not issued by a trusted CA, such as a self-signed certificate. When your client will be connecting back to a server that you control, this is a valid and effective way of securing the SSL/TLS communications link between them (and does not require you to purchase certificates from commercial CAs).

To illustrate this security model, we will configure an Android application to trust a self-signed server certificate. All other certificates, including those issued by Certificate Authorities that are normally trusted by the Android system, will be rejected and the device will not be able to establish SSL/TLS sessions with them. Everything we are doing would work just as well with a CA-issued certificate in place of a self-signed one; we would just export the certificate from the server instead of generating it ourselves, as we are about to do.

In order to set up a private client-to-server secure communications path, the first step is to install a self-signed certificate on your server's web server. There are many ways to generate such a certificate. One way uses the existing Android tools, specifically the *keytool* CLI utility. For our example, we will first use the keytool to generate the certificate, in this case for a host named *server.example.com*:

```
keytool -genkey -dname "cn=server.example.com, ou=Development, o=example.com, c=US" -
alias selfsignedcert1 -keypass genericPassword -keystore certsjks -storepass
genericPassword -validity 365
```

This command generates a certificate for the *server.example.com*, the full DNS name for the server that our Android application is going to communicate with. The `-valid ity` argument specifies that the certificate will be valid for 365 days, starting with the current day. The certificate is generated by the *keytool* utility and stored in a *keystore* that we call `certsjks`. This keystore is in the JKS format, short for Java KeyStore. You can think of a keystore as being just like a safe, with lots of different pieces of important information stored within (in this case, just one piece: our new certificate and its associated private keys). We assign a password to both the JKS keystore (this password is required to do anything with the keystore) and to the certificate itself (this password is required to export a certificate out of the keystore or to do anything else with it).

We now have a self-signed certificate in the name of *server.example.com*. At this point, we need to do two things with it. First, we need to transfer it (and its associated private keys) over to the server that will use it (*server.example.com* in this case). The exact procedure for this depends on what type of server you have, and is not really part of the Android effort, so we will not discuss it in detail here. However, we also need to install it in our Android application so that it recognizes and trusts the certificate when the server presents it. To do this, we need to get the certificate in a more usable form, because Android applications do not directly work with JKS keystores. Rather, they prefer to use BKS keystores, short for Bouncy Castle KeyStore. Bouncy Castle is a library of cryptographic routines that Android uses for much of its cryptography implementation, keystores included. So we need to get our certificate out of the JKS keystore and into a BKS keystore before we can make use of it in our Android application.

In order to create a BKS keystore with our certificate, we need to download the Bouncy Castle cryptographic provider. You can find this on the Internet by going to the Legion of the Bouncy Castle website (*http://bouncycastle.org*) and downloading the latest provider JAR files (the filename is of the format *bcproc-jdk-1-146.jar*, which is the current version as of late 2011). Once you have this file downloaded (say, in the */home/user1/ dev/lib* directory), you can use the keytool to export the self-signed certificate out of the JKS keystore and into the BKS keystore:

```
keytool -export -alias selfsignedcert1 -keystore certsjks -storepass genericPassword -
keypass genericPassword -file cert.cer

keytool -import -file cert.cer -keypass genericPassword -keystore /home/user1/dev/
project1/res/raw/selfsignedcertsbks -storetype BKS -storepass genericPassword -
providerClass org.bouncycastle.jce.provider.BouncyCastleProvider -providerpath /home/
user1/lib/bcprov-jdk16-146.jar -alias selfsignedcert1
```

The first of these two commands exports our certificate out of the JKS keystore in which we created it, into a raw certificate file, *cert.cer*. Then, using the second command, we create a new BKS keystore and import the certificate into it. Note that we need to supply the full path to the JAR file we downloaded from Bouncy Castle to complete this operation. Also, note that we assign a password to our BKS keystore, just like we did with our JKS one.

We now have our certificate in a BKS keystore. The next step will be to include that keystore within our Android app, so that we can make use of it when setting up an SSL/ TLS connection back to our server. Notice that we created the BKS keystore within an application's project directory, */home/user1/dev/project1/res/raw/*. This is a resource directory. Whatever development environment you are using (such as Eclipse with the ADK) should detect that a new raw resource has been copied there and add it to your project (after which you should see selfsignedcertsbks show up as a resource ID), allowing you to make use of it.

Now that the keystore with your certificate is available to the Android application, you need to configure the application to open SSL/TLS connections using it. This process is a little complex and requires the use of multiple objects:

KeyStore
> An object representation of a cryptographic keystore; it contains certificates and/ or private keys.

TrustManager
> An object with the responsibility of deciding whether the credentials (certificate) of another entity should be trusted and accepted for use in an SSL/TLS communication session.

TrustManagerFactory

A factory class that creates TrustManager objects to specifications provided by the caller.

SSLContext

An object that holds a list of properties concerning the SSL configuration. These typically include what client-side keys to use, what server-side certificates should be accepted (by specifying which TrustManagers to use), and where the random numbers required as part of the protocol should come from.

SSLSocketFactory

A factory class that manufactures SSL/TLS sockets based on a set of properties specified in an SSLContext.

We will now look at how to use these classes together to accomplish our goal of an SSL/TLS secure session to a server using a self-signed certificate.

First, you must create and use a KeyStore object to access the keystore that you just added as a resource. The procedure for doing so is pretty simple:

```
KeyStore selfsignedKeys = KeyStore.getInstance("BKS");
selfsignedKeys.load(context.getResources().openRawResource(R.raw.selfsignedcertsbks),
    "genericPassword".toCharArray());
```

This code reads in the raw resource that is really the BKS keystore and uses it as the KeyStore class object. Note that we need to supply the password that is used to protect the keystore (the one we set when we created the keystore) so that Android can open it and access the certificate contained inside.

Next, we create a TrustManagerFactory object and initialize it using this KeyStore. This configures the TrustManagerFactory to produce TrustManager objects based around the contents of the KeyStore. Remember that a TrustManager is used to decide whether a server's certificate should be trusted, so by building a TrustManager around the keystore that contains our self-signed certificate, we are building one that will trust the certificate. To create the TrustManagerFactory, we do the following:

```
TrustManagerFactory trustMgr =
    TrustManagerFactory.getInstance(TrustManagerFactory.getDefaultAlgorithm());
trustMgr.init(selfsignedKeys);
```

This creates a TrustManagerFactory that will produce TrustManager objects that use the default SSL/TLS algorithms (that is what the getDefaultAlgorithm() method call does) and will utilize our custom keystore, which is set in the call to init() that passes in that keystore, to decide which server certificates to trust.

Once we have the TrustManagerFactory, we can create the SSLContext that we will need to make SSL/TLS connections using our certificate:

```
SSLContext selfsignedSSLcontext = SSLContext.getInstance("TLS");
selfsignedSSLcontext.init(null, trustMgr.getTrustManagers(), new SecureRandom());
HttpsURLConnection.setDefaultSSLSocketFactory(
    selfsignedSSLcontext.getSocketFactory());
```

The call to `init()` takes three parameters: the sources of the client-side keys used, the sources of trust, and the sources of randomness. As we are not doing SSL/TLS where the server authenticates the client but only where the client authorizes the server, we do not need to supply the first parameter and just pass `null`. The second parameter is where we supply the `TrustManagerFactory`'s generated `TrustManager` list. Because the `TrustManagerFactory` was configured to utilize the keystore we created that has only the self-signed certificate in question, this new `SSLContext` will accept only our certificate and no others, not even the normally accepted CA-signed certificates. Since our goal here is a private client/server secure communications path, this is fine (indeed, this is exactly what we want; consider the Principle of Least Privilege). The third parameter is how the random numbers necessary for SSL/TLS are generated; here we use a new `SecureRandom` instance.

Finally, the static method `setDefaultSSLSocketFactory()` of the `HttpsURLConnection` class is called. This method changes the `SSLSocketFactory` used to create new SSL/TLS connections. This line creates an `SSLSocketFactory` based on our `SSLContext` and then configures the `HttpsURLConnection` class to use it, so that all of the parameters we have set—the trust of our self-signed certificate—are utilized. From this point forward, any SSL/TLS connections created from our application will use this new configuration and, therefore, can only be made to our server and nowhere else:

```
URL serverURL = new URL("https://server.example.com/endpointTest");
HttpsURLConnection serverConn = (HttpsURLConnection)serverURL.openConnection();
```

 We have just discussed how a decision is made concerning the trusting of the certificate presented by the server. Keep in mind that two checks are made during the set up of an SSL/TLS connection: certificate trust and hostname verification. Even if we configure the SSL/TLS environment for our application to trust a self-signed certificate, the hostname verification checks are still made, so the name on the certificate must still match the name of the host to which we are trying to connect in order for the connection to be set up. If we are using a self-signed certificate that has a different name, a custom `HostnameVerifier` may need to be configured as we discussed previously. This should be avoided if possible, because hostname verification checks are important to make sure we are talking to the server that we think we are.

One Step Further: Using Client-Side Authentication SSL/TLS

So far, we have seen how to modify the SSL/TLS configuration for an application by changing its TrustManagers so that it would trust specific certificates. This had two major effects. First, it allowed the Android application—the client—to trust a self-signed certificate on the server, something the default SSL/TLS configuration would not do. Second, it forced the Android application to trust a certificate *only* from the server it would be talking to (since that is the only one we put in the keystore that the `TrustManagerFactory` is initialized with). This allows the client to know that it really is talking with the server that it thinks it is, and that the communications between them are protected with strong encryption. This is a great start to a secure communications channel.

However, there is still one hole in this solution: the server has not yet authenticated the client, so while the client knows that it is talking to the server it wants to, the server has no assurances that it is talking to the client that it wants to. In a controlled environment, such as a company application that logs in employees and lets them conduct sensitive operations or read proprietary information, the server may want to make sure that only authorized devices are getting in. Hence the need for client-side authentication in SSL/TLS.

We will now implement such a solution. We will extend our previous example of trusting self-signed server certificates to provide client certificates to the server as well. Note that to require clients that connect using SSL/TLS to present a certificate and to specify which certificates are to be accepted requires configuration on the server. This part of the process is beyond the scope of this book, largely because the process can vary greatly depending on which type of web server you are going to be communicating with. For now, let's assume that you have this set up on your server and you have a client certificate that you are ready to deploy into the Android application. We will further assume that you have that client certificate in a BKS format keystore, named clientauthcertsBKS, and you still have the selfsignedcertsBKS keystore containing the server certificate. Starting with these two keystores, we will create our client for mutually authenticated SSL/TLS, with only specific server certificates trusted.

Just as before, we need to create a KeyStore object to access the BKS keystores that are included in the project. First, we will set up the TrustManagerFactory that we need to ensure that we are talking only to the servers we want to. This is the exact same code as in the previous section:

```
KeyStore selfsignedKeys = KeyStore.getInstance("BKS");
selfsignedKeys.load(context.getResources().openRawResource(R.raw.selfsignedcertsbks),
  "genericPassword".toCharArray());
TrustManagerFactory trustMgr =
    TrustManagerFactory.getInstance(TrustManagerFactory.getDefaultAlgorithm());
trustMgr.init(selfsignedKeys);
```

Now we will perform largely the same process, but we need to create a KeyManager instead of a TrustManager. KeyManager objects represent our own credentials (certificates) that can be supplied to a server for purposes of client-side authentication in SSL/TLS. The procedure is analogous to a TrustManager, in that we create a KeyManagerFactory based on the KeyStore object holding the certificates:

```
KeyStore clientauthKeys = KeyStore.getInstance("BKS");
clientauthKeys.load(context.getResources().openRawResource(R.raw.clientauthcertsbks),
  "genericPassword".toCharArray());
KeyManagerFactory keyMgr =
    KeyManagerFactory.getInstance(KeyManagerFactory.getDefaultAlgorithm());
keyMgr.init(clientauthKeys, "genericPassword".toCharArray());
```

Similar to when we were creating a `TrustManagerFactory`, this creates a `KeyManagerFactory` that will produce `KeyManager` objects that use the default SSL/TLS algorithms (that is what the `getDefaultAlgorithm()` method call does) and will utilize our custom keystore—which is set in the call to `init()` that passes in that keystore—to decide which client certificates to provide to servers that require client-side authentication. Note that in this case, we need to supply the keystore password to the `init()` function, as we will be using the private keys associated with the certificates, something that we did not have to do when dealing with a `TrustManager`.

Now we have a `TrustManagerFactory` to generate `TrustProvider` objects that will accept certificates included in our keystore when they are provided by a server we connect to (the self-signed certificate in this case). We also have a `KeyManagerFactory` to generate `KeyManager` objects that will provide client certificates that we can use to identify ourselves to those servers. With these, we can create the `SSLContext` that we will need to make SSL/TLS connections.

```
SSLContext privateSSLcontext = SSLContext.getInstance("TLS");
privateSSLcontext.init(keyMgr.getKeyManagers(), trustMgr.getTrustManagers(),
    new SecureRandom());
HttpsURLConnection.setDefaultSSLSocketFactory(privateSSLcontext.getSocketFactory());
```

Recall that the call to `init()` takes three parameters: the sources of the client-side keys used, the sources of trust, and the sources of randomness. This time, we are doing client-side authentication, so we include our `KeyManager` objects as the first parameter. We then include our `TrustManager` list as the second parameter. Finally, as the third parameter is how the random numbers necessary for SSL/TLS are generated; here we use a new `SecureRandom` instance.

And that's it. We now have an SSL/TLS configuration that restricts which server certificates we will accept (the contents of the `selfsignedcertsbks` keystore) and includes client certificates that we can use to identify ourselves to those servers (the contents of the `clientauthcertsbks` keystore). By making use of these constructs, we can fully specify how we want our SSL/TLS communications to act for our application. The ability to specify both who we are willing to talk to and to whom we will identify ourselves allows the creation of private, secure communication tunnels that are both mutually authenticated and encrypted, ideal for the world of Android client applications communicating with servers.

```
URL serverURL = new URL("https://server.example.com/mutualauth_endpointTest");
HttpsURLConnection serverConn = (HttpsURLConnection)serverURL.openConnection();
```

Threats Against Devices Using Data in Transit

Aside from the confidentiality of the data that our app may be transmitting or receiving, the app needs to be able to defend itself against rogue data submitted to it. As the developer of a mobile app, you are writing code that runs locally on a device, and the inputs to that app may be very tightly controlled. You probably accept input from the user in the form of the screen and/or keyboard. You may accept input over the network from other entities that communicate with you. You may also read data stored on the filesystem that you previously read. In all of these cases, however, you need to account for attackers that may be able to mount their dastardly deeds by manipulating those inputs to your app. Web application developers need to be extremely concerned about proper input validation because malicious input that you fail to catch can lead to dangerous vulnerabilities such as SQL injection (or other command injection), cross-site scripting attacks, and exploitation of buffer overflows. Client applications, including Android applications, are not as susceptible to these types of attacks, but they are not immune either. As an application developer, Android or iOS, client-side or server-side, you need to be aware of the need for proper input validation and the consequences if you do not properly perform it. This is truly the primary tenant of application security today.

The primary programming flaw in most of today's applications is a lack of proper input validation. Applications trust that the input that is provided to them is what they expect. After all, if you ask a user to supply a username that is between four and eight characters, do you think that they will provide anything else? Even if you do, would you think that instead of meeting that criteria, they would supply ten thousand characters instead? You may very well not. But a failure to consider such a case can give rise to a classic problem in application security: the buffer overflow. Now, Java (and this includes Android) applications are much harder to exploit using buffer overflow attacks, but it is still possible. Other vulnerabilities beyond buffer overflows exist as well. This leads to our primary point of this section: never blindly trust input into your application; validate anything before you process it.

 The primary tenant of application security is very simple. Do not trust any input into your application. Validate it first, then process it.

Let's look at an example of *SQL injection*, which is one specific (but the most prevalent) form of a class of vulnerabilities known as *command injection*. In this type of vulnerability, input from an outside source is used directly as part of a command, in this case a SQL expression that is passed to a database interpreter. For example, consider a case where the user supplies a username and password to an application, which must then verify that the combination is valid to allow access. (This is not a very clear example for a client application, like most apps running on an Android device will be, but many such apps do have databases that may be issued queries with parameters based on inputs, so this is a very real-world example.) In such a case, a typical SQL statement that would be issued by the application to the database would be:

```
String loginQuery = "SELECT * FROM useraccounts WHERE userID = '" +
    request.getParameter("userID") + "' AND password = '" +
    request.getParameter("password") + "'";
```

In this example, you can see that the application forms a SQL statement that is designed to see whether the submitted user ID and password are valid. However, if whoever is submitting the information were to submit these values:

```
userID   = ' or 1=1 --
password = doesNotMatter
```

The resulting query that would be supplied to the SQL database interpreter would be:

```
SELECT * FROM useraccounts WHERE userID = '' or 1=1 -- AND password='doesNotMatter'
```

This SQL statement would then evaluate and return all of the data from the user accounts table, as the WHERE condition would always be true (due to the OR 1=1 condition) and the password checking clause would be commented out.

This unintended behavior is made possible because of two primary problems. First, our app did not properly validate the input that was received before using that input to form the SQL statement to be submitted to the database interpreter. Second, the problem is enabled because when query strings are constucted in such a manner, the database system cannot tell the difference between code and data; the initial apostrophe (') submitted in the userID is actually data, but is being interpreted as code because the database cannot tell that it should be interpreted as a literal data value.

What are the lessons here? First, SQL injection is one type of vulnerability that is made possible when proper input validation is not performed. Expanding on this, rather than look for each specific vulnerability, developers must take one very simple concept to heart and consider it when writing the portions of their application that deal with processing input, regardless of where is it received from. All input is not to be trusted and must be validated before it is used in any way. You, as an application developer, have no control over what is going on outside of your application. You do not control the device's operating system, you do not control the wireless base station that the device is communicating with, and you do not control any of the routers that the data going to, or from, the device passes through. Due to this, you must consider any incoming communications to be hostile and maliciously tampered with, so you must properly validate and/or sanitize them before you use them, to protect your application.

Second, database calls where the entire SQL statement that will be sent to the database is composed of text concatenated together, mixing commands and data, is dangerous. Indeed, SQL injection attacks cannot be fully mitigated by input validation because sometimes dangerous inputs (such as the apostrophe, in the case of SQL) may also be valid inputs (think of an application that asks for a name and someone that has an Irish name that contains this character). In this case, it is critical to separate the command/control portions of the query from the data that is used to construct it. Luckily, the database programming methodology of Android (really, of Java) provides a means to accomplish this. So, let's move on and discuss these two lessons in greater detail. First, we will explore input validation and then move on to safe database interaction.

Input Validation: The Central Tenant of Application Security

As we have seen, all input to our application must be considered untrusted and must be checked before we can use it. We have already explored strategies to ensure that the data we have received did, in fact, come from the entity we expected it to. We have also seen complementary ways to make sure we are sending data to the entity we think we are sending it to. But even if our app accepts data from anywhere, or we have nothing but absolute trust in the entity we are accepting input from, we must validate that data. To that end, there are two primary approaches and we will discuss both of them here.

Reject-Known-Bad

Reject-Known-Bad is a type of input validation where the app will look for inputs that contain data known to be bad, and reject them. For example, in the case of SQL injection that we discussed before, the exploit input worked because it contained a ' that terminates a string in SQL. If an application were to look at all submitted input and reject any input that included such a character, it would be implementing a Reject-Known-Bad input validation strategy. Along similar lines, if a developer were to write an HTTP form submission routine that processed a comment to a website, he may want to look for inputs that include script tags and reject any such inputs. Looking for known-exploit inputs like this is a staple of Reject-Known-Bad input validation.

Such techniques are weak. This is largely because the set of possibly bad inputs is infinite. As each new attack technique or variation is discovered, the list of known-bad inputs would need to be updated. This *blacklist* would quickly be unsustainable, as each developer would need to keep their apps' input validation routines up-to-date with each new discovery. In addition, examining each input submitted to an application for each and every known-bad string would require extensive processing of each input string and this would slow down such an application considerably. This is not a sustainable, nor desirable, strategy for input validation.

Accept-Known-Good

A better technique for input validation is *Accept-Known-Good*, where an application looks for inputs that it does expect and rejects all other inputs that do not fit that specification. This is sometimes known as *positive validation* or *whitelisting*. Here, each input is checked for a number of criteria:

Data Type
  Is the data received of the type expected?

Length
  Is the data received the correct length?

Numeric Range
  If the data is numeric, is it in the expected range?

Numeric Sign
    If the data is numeric, is it of the correct sign?

Syntax/Grammar
    Is the data in the correct syntax?

Only if received data meets all of these criteria should it be accepted and processed. If it fails any of these criteria, it should be rejected and discarded.

Another important concept in input validation is *sanitization*. This refers to the idea of changing an input into an acceptable and safe format rather than just choosing to accept or reject it. Just as in an accept-or-reject approach, sanitization can be done using either a whitelist or blacklist approach; the same evaluation of the two approaches and the clear superiority of the accept-known-good solution applies to sanitization just as much as it does for the accept/reject approach.

Policies for Handling Erroneous Input

This brings up another question. If illegal input keeps coming in, how many times do you let the user (or whatever the application is communicating with over the network) resubmit it, and when do you terminate the application? This is another decision that must be made based on risk analysis. You don't want to let illegal input keep being retried, but you don't want to cut off legitimate users who are just messing up either. The more sensitive the data being processed by the application, the quicker you will want to stop accepting input if each attempt is illegal.

Wrapping It Up: Input Validation

Input validation is the key component of application security. Applications rely on inputs—data that arrives from outside of the application—to drive actions and direct the application what to do. One of the primary problems in applications is that developers trust that input. Remember that any piece of data submitted from outside your app can be submitted by, or manipulated by, an attacker. You need to verify that the data received by your application is valid and safe to process. We have seen two approaches to doing so: looking for things that you know are bad and excluding those inputs, and looking for things that you know are good and accepting only those inputs. We have demonstrated that the second approach is vastly superior.

Preventing Command Injection

As we have seen, input validation is a critical part of protecting any application from attack. However, as we also discussed recently, it is necessary but not sufficient. Input validation only verifies that inputs are what we think they should be. There may be situations (indeed, there often are) where valid inputs are dangerous when used in certain ways. To go back to the example we used previously, suppose we accept a person's name as input. To properly allow certain names, such as many Irish names, we need to allow apostrophes in such inputs. However, if we use such inputs to form SQL statements, we are exposing our application to SQL injection attacks. This occurs because when we simply combine the command portions of our statements with the data portions using string concatenation, there is no way for the database to determine which is command and which is code, so data may be misinterpreted as code, leading to the attacks. Luckily, there is a way to separate the commands from the data when interacting with the database. A slight alteration to the way we write database statements can prevent SQL injection attacks.

Looking at an example similar to the earlier one, let's consider looking up a user's last name in a database. The unsafe way to form this statement looks something like this:

```
SQLiteDatabase db = dbHelper.getWriteableDatabase();
String userQuery = "SELECT lastName FROM useraccounts WHERE userID = "
    + request.getParameter("userID");
SQLiteStatement prepStatement = db.compileStatement(userQuery);
String userLastname = prepStatement.simpleQueryForString();
```

In this example, we first form the SQL query that will be sent to the database by concatenating command instructions with data taken from the network request. This is unsafe as we do not know what the network request contains and even if we have performed input validation at this point (which we absolutely should have), dangerous characters may be part of the whitelist. So the input could still be dangerous to send to a SQL-based database in this manner. What we need is a way to separate the command from the data. Here is the proper way to perform such a query against the database, where the command is separated from the data:

```
SQLiteDatabase db = dbHelper.getWriteableDatabase();
String userQuery = "SELECT lastName FROM useraccounts WHERE userID = ?";
SQLiteStatement prepStatement = db.compileStatement(userQuery);
prepStatement.bindString(1, request.getParameter("userID"));
String userLastname = prepStatement.simpleQueryForString();
```

By taking advantage of the compileStatement capability, we can effectively separate commands from data in SQL statements, by using the ? marker. This is known as a *parameterized query*, as the query string includes placeholders (question marks) to mark the data and the values for those pieces of data are filled in independently (by the bindString() call in our example). When we employ this capability, the database can separate command from data. Even if the userID input were to contain an apostrophe, the database would know that it is part of the data and treat it as data, looking for results in the database that include that character, as opposed to treating it as part of the command, which would give rise to a SQL injection attack. As a general rule, whenever your application is interacting with a database, you should use parameterized queries. A SQL statement should never be formed by concatenating command and data together.

Any interactions with SQL-based databases should always use parameterized queries. You should never form a statement by concatenating command and data together, because the database would not be able to differentiate between the two.

CHAPTER 7

Summary

Way back in Chapter 1, we talked about what this book would be and why you, as a developer, would want to read it. This book has had a single purpose: to educate developers who are writing applications for the Android platform on how to write those applications to be more secure and robust in the face of attack. We've touched on a number of points along the way, so let's quickly summarize the primary themes we have seen and wrap this book up.

Key Themes

It's All About Risk

If there has been one primary topic that I hope to have conveyed, it is that security—application security or otherwise—is really risk management. Without the context of risk, security means nothing. When you hear someone say that their application, system, or building is secure, you should immediately think, "Secure against what?" What are the threats that the security features of this system designed to protect against? What are the vulnerabilities that this system may have? And what would be the consequences if one of those vulnerabilities were to be exploited? Until you know the answers to those questions, you cannot judge just how secure anything is. For a typical home in suburban America, you may have good deadbolt locks, strong construction, and a home security system, and you would be pretty secure against most common threats, such as burglary. You are not, however, in any way secure against more exotic threats, such as an attack by a 30-foot tall monster. What are the threats, vulnerabilities, and consequences? If the risk that comes out of your risk analysis is high, you need to mitigate it. If the risk that comes out of your risk analysis is low, then you are OK. But every security feature you deploy should be appropriate based on the risk.

The Principle of Least Privilege

Another primary topic that I hope you've understood well is the Principle of Least Privilege. Basically, entities should have just enough privileges to do their job and no more. If your application does not need to have Internet access, do not request the Internet permission. If you want to make your Content Provider available to other applications on a device, but only you should be able to update the data, make sure you configure separate read and write permissions on that entity. Along very similar lines, store only the data that you need to do your job. If your application does not need to know users' bank account numbers, do not ask for them. If your application uses passwords to encrypt some sensitive data, and you never need to supply that password anywhere else, store a hashed version (actually, a version that has gone through the PBE algorithms we discussed that use multiple hash rounds and salt) instead of the actual password. Run with only the minimum privileges you need.

Use the Permissions System

Android offers a very robust and extensive permissions system. If you use any features of the system that are deemed dangerous, you need to declare that, and the user needs to confirm your access. You can also use permissions to craft a robust access control strategy around all of the components of your application, as we spent Chapter 4 discussing. If your application handles sensitive data, use this feature. Lock down access to all of your components, so that they can be used only as you intend them to be. This is why the permissions model exists, so use it.

Android Is an Open Architecture

The Android architecture is based on some time-tested components, and the Linux kernel it uses is central to the isolation provided to applications. Android, however, is also an open platform and it is trivial to obtain root-level access to an Android device, much easier than on any other major mobile platform. Do not ignore this consideration; make sure you fully understand the environment your applications will be running in. If you need to store some sensitive data, make sure that it is protected at a level appropriate for the risk involved.

Get the Cryptography Right

In order to protect sensitive data to the level warranted by the risk, you will often need to employ encryption, so make sure you use the Android-provided libraries and use them correctly. If you need to send or receive sensitive data over the network, make sure you use an appropriately configured SSL/TLS system. But, whatever you end up doing, make sure you use what is out there and do not attempt to craft your own solutions or implementations. Cryptography, and the protection of sensitive information in general, is a very complex topic with lots of subtle points that can easily reduce its effectiveness by huge amounts, so be careful.

Never Trust User Input

We got to this late in the book, as it is a topic that has historically been primarily a concern for server and service coding. However, the same principles apply here. If you accept input from anywhere outside of your application, whether from the user on the device or from over the network, you cannot trust it to be what you think it is. We walked through a simple example of SQL injection, and that was just the beginning of all of the vulnerabilities that exist due to a lack of solid input validation. Always check your input to make sure it is what you expect it to be, no more and no less, before you begin to process it. Always.

Wrapping It Up

I sincerely hope that you have learned a lot from this book. The previous section outlines many of what I consider key takeaways; I hope that these key points have been made clear and that you can benefit from the wisdom contained therein. Application security is an extensive topic and this book has served as more of an introduction than anything else. But it does contain real, practical, actionable knowledge that you can put to use right away while developing Android applications. It would be wonderful if everyone that read this book came away with a good understanding of these principles and a strong desire to learn more. If you have, then welcome to the application security discipline. If not, that's fine too. Take what you've learned and apply it in your development efforts moving forward. Mobile development is where the future lies, for now. Make sure it's a positive, robust, and more secure world.

About the Author

Jeff Six is a senior security engineer at a major financial institution based in Baltimore, Maryland, where he works to secure customer and firm data. A major component of Jeff's job is working with developers to enhance the security of applications through education, code reviews, and deployment of modern application security techniques and frameworks. He also develops security-related applications, primarily using the Java EE platform. Prior to this position and a comparable one at another financial services firm, Jeff worked at the National Security Agency on similar application security projects and development efforts, focused on information assurance. Jeff has been a member of the Adjunct Faculty at the University of Delaware since 2000, teaching an object-oriented programming with Java course for ten years and, more recently, a course on Secure Software Design. He has been a lifeguard since 1993, and an instructor since 1995. Additionally, Jeff is an amateur triathlete, competing at the sprint, Olympic, and 70.3 distances.

Get even more for your money.

Join the O'Reilly Community, and register the O'Reilly books you own. It's free, and you'll get:

- $4.99 ebook upgrade offer
- 40% upgrade offer on O'Reilly print books
- Membership discounts on books and events
- Free lifetime updates to ebooks and videos
- Multiple ebook formats, DRM FREE
- Participation in the O'Reilly community
- Newsletters
- Account management
- 100% Satisfaction Guarantee

Signing up is easy:

1. **Go to: oreilly.com/go/register**
2. **Create an O'Reilly login.**
3. **Provide your address.**
4. **Register your books.**

Note: English-language books only

To order books online:
oreilly.com/store

For questions about products or an order:
orders@oreilly.com

To sign up to get topic-specific email announcements and/or news about upcoming books, conferences, special offers, and new technologies:
elists@oreilly.com

For technical questions about book content:
booktech@oreilly.com

To submit new book proposals to our editors:
proposals@oreilly.com

O'Reilly books are available in multiple DRM-free ebook formats. For more information:
oreilly.com/ebooks

O'REILLY®

Spreading the knowledge of innovators   oreilly.com

The information you need, when and where you need it.

With Safari Books Online, you can:

Access the contents of thousands of technology and business books

- Quickly search over 7000 books and certification guides
- Download whole books or chapters in PDF format, at no extra cost, to print or read on the go
- Copy and paste code
- Save up to 35% on O'Reilly print books
- **New!** Access mobile-friendly books directly from cell phones and mobile devices

Stay up-to-date on emerging topics before the books are published

- Get on-demand access to evolving manuscripts.
- Interact directly with authors of upcoming books

Explore thousands of hours of video on technology and design topics

- Learn from expert video tutorials
- Watch and replay recorded conference sessions

O'REILLY®

Ingram Content Group UK Ltd.
Milton Keynes UK
UKHW030615080323
418199UK00007B/369

9 781449 315078